Count Your Blessings

Short stories and poems of identity and hope

Fiona Linday

O&U
Onwards & Upwards

Onwards and Upwards Publishers

4 The Old Smithy
London Road
Rockbeare
EX5 2EA
United Kingdom.
www.onwardsandupwards.org

Copyright © Fiona Linday 2021

The moral right of Fiona Linday to be identified as the author of this work has been asserted by the author in accordance with the Copyright, Designs and Patents Act 1988.

All rights reserved.

No part of this publication may be reproduced or transmitted in any form or by any means, electronic or mechanical, including photocopy, recording or any information storage and retrieval system, without permission in writing from the author or publisher.

First edition, published in the United Kingdom by Onwards and Upwards Publishers Ltd. (2021).

ISBN: 978-1-78815-615-8
Typeface: Sabon LT

Some of these stories are based on true events. Where this occurs, names and identifying details have been changed to protect the privacy of individuals.

Contents

Introduction 5
God's Family 7
Off the Beaten Track 8
Do You Want to Know a Secret? 19
Still First 21
Back and Beyond 27
Paradise Lost... Not! 32
Meg's Diary 40
Finding Myself as the Tide Turns 46
The Blessings of Cotgrave Colliery in Our Back Yard 54
Lord, My King and My God 57
The Real Me 59
Love 73
Rosy 77
By the Grace of God Go Eye 79
Our Picasso Dish 84
A Dot Deaf Legacy 85
Family Ties Go Beyond Token Gestures 89
A Delicately Laced Fingerprint 93
A Veteran Finds His Best Mate 96
The Last Post – Turning Over a New Leaf 104
Going Full Circle 107
My 'New Normal' Schedule 109
Surviving Groundhog Day with the Cross 117
Horses for Courses – A Letter to my Younger Self 119

Also by Fiona Linday 121
About the Author 122

Count Our Blessings

2022

To Dorothy,
Merry Christmas,
Fiona

Introduction

We Are Nearly There

This book shows how creative writing has helped me express difficult and important issues over the last two decades. Over the years, family and friends have given much good advice most of which I've taken with a pinch of salt. Now, as I attempt to answer my grandchildren's questions, I realise that I should have paid much more attention. In this book for a crossover audience, I hope that the scenarios at many stages of my journey are like salt to the reader. I trust that my experiences might resonate with some of their own life challenges and that the reader finds solace in the resulting inferred solutions. Picking controversial topics to explore has helped raise awareness of several inequalities. I have often taken part in the active learner challenge; authentically writing alongside inclusive, vocational learners. Maybe I should have valued these words spoken to me as a teenager:

"Just because you have paper qualifications doesn't mean you know anything!"

"Think before you speak!" (or write!)

With that in mind, I trust the reader will feel free to browse through these inspirational thoughts in poetry and short story created as a collection from my life. There is more than a hint of truth in these tales about the need to belong, which are ordered either by when they were published or the age of the protagonist. (By the way, in the narrative the muse is not always me!) As you may notice, at least one protagonist is male so that is a comment from observing others. Primarily, my thought-provoking work has settings around the East Midlands but reflects times spent abroad, too. I've had the great privilege to read and perform my words to a wide audience. Thus, I'm delighted to gain a concluding home for these words. Enjoy dipping in and out of my stories.

I am grateful for the support of family and friends. This work excludes text for younger children but acknowledges areas where children have enlightened my path. My intention is to collate these short stories punctuating them with poetry. Thanks go to all those who believe these pieces of prose are worth recording and for an Almighty Father who sustains me.

God's Family

Thanks, Lord God, that in the beginning
You blessed us with our fantastic world
Then you chose us to be in your precious family
Next, you said, "See eye to eye,
Live hand in hand, work shoulder to shoulder,
Serve and pray daily and
Be a true family for Me"

Thanks, Lord God, for sending us Jesus
To show us the way, truth and life
Then you gave us the bible to study
You encouraged us to "Forgive one another
Like sister and brother, love unconditionally
Belong to our church and
Give all the glory to Me"

Thanks, Lord God, that life will not end
When we believe wholeheartedly
Though we're tired, you'll always be our special friend
You gently remind us, "Keep seeking my face,
Stay in my will, live by My grace,
Claim the room reserved, when your time is done and
Come, open heaven's gates to Me"[1]

---

[1] Published in 'God's Wonderful World'; Pierrepont-Gamston Primary School; *The School Book, 2006.*

Off the Beaten Track

SNALDOV, THE BALTICS AND ME. WE JUST DON'T seem to fit. Since all the trouble, I've changed. I know it's me because I don't feel part of anything anymore.

It all seems safe here but things aren't always what they seem.

From where I stand I can see twenty-two bullet holes in the wall of our house. Mrs. Ivanova, across the road, has only fifteen. I counted them.

Yes! That's thirty-seven bullets that missed.

I came out here for fresh air but there's no fresh air, only mud. But that's okay.

One day this mud will be a meadow of tall buttercups. I know it.

Right now, though, I have to collect the eggs.

I despise those chickens. I despise the way they're turning our yard into a grey, slippery mess. It's horrible. Still, the eggs are lovely.

When I look out over the huddled rooftops that seem to squash me, I think of Branimir and my eyes follow the pillars of smoke that drift over the village to the hills.

Branimir is in those hills, with his family. They're gypsies and no one likes gypsies, except me. I really like Branimir. His smile does it for me. When I'm with him everything seems safe.

I met him last summer, a summer that went on forever. The sun excited the whole hillside until the flowers, the trees, the bushes and the grass all burst into colour.

Then a bundle of feathers dropped from the roof, startling me.

"Stupid creature!" I shouted.

Off the Beaten Track

I want Branimir. I want his life and his freedom. And I want it now.

But this is my life. Chickens, mud and my dad, Konstantin.

I hate my dad.

I didn't always hate him. A long time ago we used to have great fun together.

He was always laughing, always ready for a game. At bedtime he'd tuck me in and read me this story, the same one every night. It's like the bible story about the child, Isaac, being given back to God by Abraham, his dad. Only instead of Isaac being saved in this story, the boy gets turned into gold. I don't trust my dad. I used to love him but that was then.

And this is now.

In our house we only have five rooms for eight of us and my dad fills them all. I share a bedroom with my sister but the boys are really cramped in their room, top to toe in two beds. The front room's full of Dad's mysterious boxes and we're not allowed in there. If I so much as touch the door he yells, "You, girl. Here! Now," and I dread that.

I yell back, "I have got a name, you know! I'm Yuliya, Yuliya."

That's when he gives me a smack round the head.

"Bring it on, Yuliya," he jeers.

I don't care what he says. I won't cry because there's no point.

So, anyway, I quite enjoy my boiled egg for breakfast, sometimes with fresh bread but not always.

My mum left for work before I was up. It was still dark when I heard the latch of the back door. She does her best. She has lots of jobs. It was freezing cold this morning and I needed to check on her because I wanted to know if Dad had done a "Bring it on, Elena" on her, too. But she seemed okay. She wasn't limping, anyway.

For some strange reason she hasn't given up on my dad yet, so neither should I.

I get up and put on layers of clothes but as Mum's already filled the stove burner, I warm myself by the oven before heading outside.

I do the chickens and see to the goats. Boring! Luckily, Lala likes to milk them.

Next, I go to Mila our horse. I love Mila. When all that's done, I come in to get warm again and put some eggs on to boil, making sure I'm washed before I shout for the boys. Then I grab my coat quickly before the rush and see how Lala's doing, poor kid. Lala's only six, so I help her dress. Lastly, I make sure she gets some breakfast.

"Hurry up, let's go see the icy cobwebs," I say and off Lala skips in front of me.

I leave my brothers to sort themselves out. They get to me with their pushing and shoving and all Dragomir hears from them is moaning: "It's not fair. Stop bossing us about! Who do you think you are?"

Dragomir always says, "I am older than you, that's what! Now, have you got all your school stuff?"

Even from where we are standing, we hear the back door slam, and then they're off.

We can even hear Dad yelling, "Some of us are still sleeping! Be quiet now!"

Then the boys, with their bags thrown over their shoulders, come running up behind us.

Well, they get to school eventually, most of the time.

At school, Mrs. Gamizov, my teacher, fills our heads with dreams of wealth and says, "Work hard, Yuliya, to get into college."

Off the Beaten Track

"Do you mean me?" I ask. "Get into college! Sofia's miles away and we've no money."

This woman can't be in her right mind.

She tries again. "It's not a problem if you find funding, Yuliya."

What a joke. The only way I could get to college would be if our church paid but they give to us already and I'm not special like the pretty stained-glass window that needs repairing. Any spare money goes there first. The bullets caught our beautiful church too and there wasn't much left inside by the time the police had finished.

But college would be brilliant.

Branimir doesn't need to go to college. He's learning on the job. His dad tells him all about horses and how to stay out of trouble. He can already catch rabbits with the dogs and shoot pheasants. His dad spends hours and hours with him.

It's Dragomir who tries to show my brothers how to do things properly but sometimes they just copy Dad and then I feel sorry for Dragomir.

Weekdays we all have to help out at home. Before dark I collect Lala, get home, dump my bag and pull on old clothes. Then I feed and lock the animals away.

Tonight, Dad blocked the fire.

"Dad, guess what?" I say. "I've been talking to Mrs. Gamizov and she thinks I could go to college."

He grinned. "Does she, ha?" I can see he's not listening to me.

But I plough on. "If I did go, I could get a good job and you wouldn't have to work for *them* anymore."

I meant his friends, those thugs. Big mistake. Dad's eyes narrowed. "Who do you think you are, Miss?" he roars, grabbing a log from the stove log pile and throwing it at me. I didn't see it coming and it hit me.

"Hey!" I cried. "What was that for?" Why did I open my big mouth?

Dad started shouting, "You don't know you're born! Where do you think the money comes from round here, stupid?"

I had to admit it was a crack shot but it hurt me. I felt a sharp pain on my cheek bone and then felt a trickle down my face. I put my hand up and it came away covered in blood.

I'd had enough, wiping the blood away. Pulling up my hood I stumbled into the yard where Mila was waiting, her hay net empty. I knew I should fill it but instead, I patted her, holding her tight. I could trust Mila. She always lets me get close. I tugged the bailer twine to let some hay tumble into the stable and, head down, she tucked in, her breath all foggy in the cold night air.

"We deserve better than him," I raged.

My brother shouted, "Supper time, Yuliya," so after a while, I went in. As usual Mum was in the kitchen pretending we were normal.

A loud bang on the back door told me Dad's friends had arrived, bringing a waft of cold air and the smell of cheap vodka with them.

"How can Dad let these creeps in?" I asked Mum.

"Shush, Yuliya," Mum said. Then, "Welcome," and there she was offering them our supper.

But after that Mum ignored them until, "How old is this one?" the guy flashing the gold tooth leered.

"Please, leave the child alone," my mum snapped. "Yuliya, it's late. Put those little ones to bed for me."

Off the Beaten Track

How I wished I could tell that old goat to get out of our house.

My brothers, being streetwise, had already gone upstairs so I tucked Lala up, then read her a quick story, giving her my half-eaten chocolate bar. Next thing we hear is a police siren and chairs crashing below. We all heard the rush for the back door as the police banged on the front, followed by dogs barking.

I can't stand this.

I knew the police were after the fake CDs Dad was selling off our horse and cart. He was handy and looked so innocent shifting loads. What worried me was the other stuff he was selling. I hoped they all got caught. My dad said, "Those police are fools," and Dragomir added, "They couldn't even catch a cold!"

I knew where that came from. It was my dad talking.

Later, I tiptoed downstairs. "Are you alright, Mum? Why does Dad keep getting us into trouble?"

"I don't know," she said, as she tidied and picked up chairs. "I just don't know, Yuliya. It's not fair, it's one thing or another. First, it was the Imperialists messing him about; now it's these black leather mobsters who have their hands on him."

All I could think was, *someone, PLEASE help us.*

Our church had tried to help us, although their sharing of bread and beautifully decorated Easter eggs wasn't as helpful as getting us away from these men would be. All the same, church prayers had held our family together. So far.

"I'll go see what's happening," I told Mum, but what I hadn't realised was that the goat was still outside, his gold tooth catching the light. I tried to get out of his way but I was too late. He grabbed me by the throat and caught my sore cheek.

"Ouch!" I yelped.

"Shut it!" he growled.

He got so close to me I could smell his breath. It stank.

"I'm going to have you!" he promised.

"Shove off!" I shouted, and somehow, I wriggled free.

When I got back inside I wanted to be sick so I rushed upstairs. Afterwards I prayed, "Lord, protect me. Please, show me a safe way out." Mum came up with cooled, recently boiled water scented with her best soap and I scrubbed myself, scrubbing away his touch. It disgusted me. My mum talked to me about forgiveness but I thought others needed that lesson far more than me. Yet, when I looked in Mum's eyes I saw a beauty no beating could ever destroy. She must have stayed with me until I managed to drop off to sleep.

After having the worst nightmares, next morning I got up as usual. Dad was keeping a low profile so he insisted I wait for the travellers.

"Go in late today, girl. Stay home whilst the horse's feet are looked at. My head's exploding! I'm going back to bed."

"It serves you right!" I whispered, but luckily he didn't hear me.

Only Branimir came today. So full of excitement, I went out. I felt guilty but why? This was my life and what I did was up to me.

"How are you today, Yuliya?" Branimir grinned.

"Good thanks, and you? Where's your dad this morning?" I asked.

"We're on the move soon," Branimir said, "so we've got lots to do but I am very glad to be here. Don't get me wrong, I love my family but you can have too much of a good thing!" He laughed, and as he brushed by me, a lovely musty smell hovered in the air.

Off the Beaten Track

"But what about you, really?" he went on.

"I'm okay," I lied but Branimir pushed my hood from my face.

"Great. Now, what's really been happening?"

"Nothing. Honest. Can I get you a hot drink?"

I tried to turn away but he took me in his arms.

"Stop right there, please, Yuliya. I'm so sorry," he stroked my face, then gently brushed the purple bruise marks on my neck. I hoped they wouldn't spoil things for us. I remembered my dream of our special day, me in a pure white wedding dress.

It made me realise how bad things had got lately. My friends regularly saw me with a black eye but Branimir hadn't, not yet. Now his gentle smile made it easy for me to trust him. So why couldn't I?

"Don't worry, I must have done it clowning around with Dragomir," I lied. His name means peaceful. I wish! Not at my house.

"Really? Well you know what Branimir means, don't you?"

"No." I couldn't help smiling.

"Branimir means protection! So if ever that's what you need, I'm your man!"

I looked into Branimir's blue eyes, then shut mine and let him kiss me. He was all I needed and even though I felt a bit wobbly, I kissed him back.

"You know I can't let this happen to you," he said. "But what I can't understand is why you have to lie about it."

"Oh, Branimir, I didn't mean to lie to you; it's just that I dream. I dream and then I hope and I pray. That's how it works with me. Otherwise, some days, I couldn't carry on."

Thoughtfully, he spoke again. "Well, when you're ready, I'll help you."

"Thanks. If only it were that easy. These people hang on once they've got you in their sights. The old goat has already threatened he's going to have me. What's worse is my dad's going to let him. It's all a waste of time." His face went red but I didn't want to get Branimir into trouble for helping me, so I went on, "Please, I really don't want to get you mixed up in this business."

"Well, it's too late, I am already involved," he said firmly, "so let me do something." He wanted to help me but I couldn't let him. I was bad news and so all we actually did was go round in circles. I pushed him away.

"I've no time for this now; I've got to get to school."

Branimir shouted me back, but I couldn't go back. All that he'd said was whirling around my head, especially the "I'm your man" part and I just couldn't say goodbye to him.

Skulking into school, my tutor didn't see me until that afternoon, when my face looked a bit better. The lessons weren't the ones I needed, like 'How to survive', and I hardly heard a word the teachers said. I got out as soon as I could.

Arriving early at the primary school gate for Lala, I was met by more stares from the parents. The boys had raced past us off home and Lala's hand in mine felt good. "Hi, Yuliya," she frowned. "Was it your turn last night?"

"Well it gave Mum a break!" I joked. "Don't ever let anyone wallop you, Lala."

"No way! I'll..."

"Shush, we'll be okay," I hoped and again, I prayed.

Usually, by home time the fire was lit but this afternoon there was no sign of smoke. Carefully, I pushed open the back door. Mum met us, out of breath. She was rushing to get Lala settled.

She whispered, "You've got to get away, Yuliya, the sooner the better. It's tonight, and it's all set up. They're

Off the Beaten Track

taking you to that Hotel Splendid. A few glamour photos by the pool and then you're his. You know the one?"

"You don't mean the old goat, with the gold tooth, Mum?" I was almost crying. "What can I do?" I panicked.

Mum went on, "It's to pay off your dad's debt. That man will trick you with a job offer because that's what happened to Mrs. Ivanova's daughter and Maria ended up in a real sorry state."

I put my head in my hands. "Darling, don't worry," my mum said. "No way would I ever let that happen to one of mine. You have to get out of his way but you won't be alone. I've asked Branimir for help. He's here now. His family know the truth and have agreed to take you with them on the road. Our families go back years, they'll help you and I know we really can trust them. They're heading over the mountains to freedom today and you're going with them." She hugged me tighter.

"Mum, I can't…"

"You'll have a future, Yuliya, you must take it!" Mum insisted.

"I don't want to leave you, I love you, Mum," I said. I couldn't believe there was hope for me, a way to be safe. I heard the back door go and there was Branimir.

"Come on, Yuliya," Branimir said, hurrying me. "There's an icy fog coming in, which will give us some good cover, so get your things together."

"I've done that, Yuliya," my mum said. "Here, take this money, it should help." Mum was one step ahead, pushing a roll of notes into my pocket. "It's what I've been saving for your college fund but you need it now. I shall pray for you."

I grabbed her hand. "I'll come back one day, Mum, I promise. Keep Dragomir out of trouble and Lala and the boys." Then I gave her a long hug. "And Dad," I added.

Carefully wrapping her shawl round me, my mum said, "I'll try. Now go!"

The gypsies' decorated carriage was in our road, waiting for me to climb on board. So this was my answered prayer. This was the way out that my mum thought was right and I chose this new life. My stomach was doing somersaults and I was so excited.

Taking Branimir's hand, I gave thanks for my second chance. For the time being I must not look back.

Finally, I felt safe.[2]

---

[2] This was written while I was mentored by Gwen Grant. It won a first prize with the local Fosseway Writers, in 2008. I read it at Shoreditch, London for Arts 4 Human Rights, 2011.

Do You Want to Know a Secret?

This question my friend often asked.
Making me wonder where exactly
that she was coming from and why
it's followed by a giggle, days past.

When paired up together in year ten
how could she really tell the truth?
As J. R. was just her nickname then
and I simply had no clue about men.

Needing pocket money meant that
Her vulnerability prevented safety.
During the babysitting trips she found
a monster lurked beneath his chat.

Hiding behind pass-me-down clothes
she moved on from being the victim.
And bravely recovered without help,
from late exams, he controlled woes.

She kept goading and even joking
My school pal never did let on to me.
She was savvy being from a big family.
Me more ignorant, I failed fathoming.

Still, she smiled even more broadly
As at last, the predator got stopped.
Relieved, I'm glad she escaped him
by applying her clear, shiny lippy.

Count Our Blessings

Lately, cooing over her male twins
as listening to 'Come on You Reds'
while working at Boots for therapy
means my secret friend now wins.[3]

---

[3] Read at Nottingham City Arts as part of their 2019 *Words for Wisdom* project.

Still First

IT WASN'T UNTIL THE ANNOYING REVERSING BEEP of the minibus echoed up our lane that I realised how late I was.

"No way. It can't be time to go already!"

The fools should come for me last. But they never listened. Half the time, I rushed so much that my skirt was tucked in my knickers. Not the look I was going for.

Their silly fault anyway, because swimming sucked.

Mum bellowed, "They're here, Bronte!"

"You don't say," I muttered. As if I'd slept through Ted knocking on our front door, like he did every other morning, except Sundays.

So I grabbed my coat and threw my bags down the stairs, where Mum tut-tutted, before passing them to Ted.

"I'm coming, keep your hair on!" I shouted.

From the forehead wavy line, Mum was not that impressed. Neither was I! Expecting me to bounce out into the black hole she called 'morning', as if it was natural. I caught sight of my awful reflection in the hall mirror. A gross, red spot blinked back at me.

Training lately was exhausting, but instead of making a fuss, I plugged into my iPod. Once on the bus, I got back to daydreaming, my absolute favourite thing.

Dreaming of a cool photo shoot and shiny hair with sparkly make-up. In these designer clothes, posing in a massive limo! That daydream wasn't mine, though, it was Emma's. She insisted on sharing.

My dream was far more doable. It was to qualify for the Paralympics. And win my race.

I put up with annoying Emma because she was a teammate. Shivering now, feeling my calf muscles plank up, I yelled, "Give us a blast with that heater, will you, Ted?" He needed to listen, or Ken would be his problem. Ken was my coach.

Emma was flicking through a fashion mag. "Want one like that one," she said, pointing randomly.

Wondering whether she meant the clothes or the body, I told her, "You should win your races, Em. That's how to earn respect."

Emma was angry. "Whatever! I wouldn't mind a piece of the action. What I can't get my head round, Bron, is that Dad thinks I've actually got a chance of bringing home a medal. Why can't he do it, if it's so important?"

"I know! It's real abuse, this World Cup training schedule," I said. "But we're the ones with pure talent." I laughed, giving her a high five.

Actually, at nearly sixteen... all I got was, "Do this, do that, more training, blah, blah!" What I really wanted was a normal life. This constant hard work got in the way.

Reality check. The minibus bumped up a curb. After the forty-minute drive, we had arrived at the sports centre.

"You know what my mum said about the Leeds Music festival, last night?" Emma blurted, as we got out of the minibus.

"Let me guess. Was it 'no', by any chance? I told you she wouldn't let you go," I smirked.

"She went on about it being too tricky in a chair. She suggested watching it on the TV! Get real! I told her I'll suss it out for myself. No probs!"

We continued up the ramp towards the Olympic-sized Loughborough Uni pool. Going through the double doors,

Emma said, "It'll be fantastic, camping." Then she went scooting off ahead.

"Whatever!" I shouted after her. "The music might be okay, too!"

Her issues were nothing, compared to my kid bro Shane. I knew that he kept skipping school and was sure that he was hiding things in his room. He needed proper sorting.

Then undressing was difficult. I was alright getting into the pool, diving down into freedom. The water was the place I could move easily, with no rules.

Muffled instructions came from Ken as I loosened off with some dolphin impressions. Not the fastest. He made me feel guilty, bitching about "giving a damn about the Paralympics".

My mate Dominic was watching. He had already been chosen for the GB medley team. He encouraged me to do laps, after the boring warm-ups. Thirty laps on my front, thirty on my back and then a good hour alternating. In the best lane, at the edge of the pool, humming 'Simply the Best', I was winning. Emma, struggling in the next lane, had her physio working on her bad leg. Looked painful, judging by her face.

"Go for the cross on the tile," Ken shouted. Timing, using passing points, kept me focused on a medal. Needing to stay in the 'can do', avoiding getting panicky, because that set off pain.

It was alright me planning adventures, when I had a date coming up I'd rather miss – going back to the dreaded Botox ward. Me, having Botox, next to big-headed girls waiting for boob jobs. Wounded, mine was free! But mine was going in my legs, to make them sturdier.

My coach said that the session went okay, despite my chilled muscles. Although my legs felt well heavy, my physio,

Laura, didn't need to do much. I heard the words "personal best", making me happy. *I did okay today.* Ken was trying to thrill me with talk of World Cup qualifiers – meaning tighter training schedules.

Getting dressed, again, without totally freezing, I thought about easier options. As we counted down to big events, the training went crazy. That explained why my constantly frizzy hair smelled of steaming chlorine.

I asked my mate Joe how his session went. Going past a group of giggly, high-pitched girls made me glad it was my legs that struggled, not my brain. Unfortunately, my brain didn't turn my legs on instantly, like those lucky dolls.

I tried to persuade waves of feeling to go further, down to my feet. Laura helped by showing me how to build up those muscles. Clever really, programming my body by stimulating my brain to increase its signalling response.

I scribbled a note to buy more hair gel. All before eight in the morning. As I arrived at school, most of my mates had just started on their day!

As I rushed to my lessons, some lads asked how it went in the elite squad. I didn't tell them much. One of Shane's mates shouted, "Where is he then, your bro?" I just shrugged. He had done several dodgy things lately. Sister's duty though, wouldn't tell.

Lovely Simon met me for lunch, asking how the session went. "Average," I said, looking for appreciation. Then, "My backstroke's getting stronger."

He nodded, trying to have a clue, and said, "Good!"

"Freestyle's my best chance," I told him. Explaining the drill Laura always gave me. Being the best that I could be, educating my muscles. "Then you're using them, not losing them!"

Simon, creeping, said, "You're perfect to me."

Still First

As we arrived at my house, Shane dared me to an arm wrestle, having all that surplus energy. "Give us a break, I'll only win!" I said. Si gave off negative waves. Shane slammed his door.

Recently, his den had weird foul pongs oozing out. Also, he'd gone loner-ish... Twenty-four/seven attached to his Playstation 'Call of Duty' games and then out cold, all day. His curtains never opened.

"He'll grow out of it," Si said.

I hoped so, missing the old bro. "Good luck, Metal Muscles," he shouted.

Maybe if I won a trophy, it would cheer him up.

So I kept pushing my body until it hurt, then Laura fixed me when I was broken. Not so easy for Shane, who needed his head fixing.

When I got back from the next final heats, Dad answered the phone, smiling. From where I was crashed, I heard "qualifiers", so I knew it was Ken.

I heard my dad say, "We were due some good news!" Then, he shouted, "So Bron, when were you going to tell us about making the G.B. squad?"

Mum had the same grin. "I knew you could do it, love," she said. "That'll mean some better funding." Then she got on the mobile to Gran.

"You make it sound amazing," I said.

Dad was dancing around our lounge. "You're on the way to London 2012, young lady! We'd better get those tickets."

But I was still thinking about Shane. I bashed his bedroom door, shouting, "You need to help me to get to the

25

Paralympics Freestyle, Shane. I CAN'T DO IT WITHOUT YOU!"[4]

---

[4] Included in *The Heavenly Road Trip* eBook with Help for Writers, 2012. In a multi-sensory performance and recorded at the Perception Exhibition, Bermondsey Project Gallery, London, 2012.

Back and Beyond

I NEVER USED TO RATE MIRACLES, BUT THE DAY I actually came back to life changed that. Forever. Now miracles are a given. The sad part was they insisted I must never tell.

"Don't ask me to keep a secret," I begged. It wasn't easy, even living at this seaside spot where nothing ever happens and no one knows anything. At first, it was like someone else's deal. As if I was no longer Talitha. Before it happened, I'd been a regular, sad sixteen-year-old.

All weekend, I'd had the worst puking bug ever. Monday started a bit dodgy, with me still feeling rubbish. My radio alarm went off, as usual. It went straight into the news. I hadn't the strength to reach to shut it up. It was some silly woman banging on about the two goals of Israel as a Jewish and democratic state, needing to coexist. As if I cared! Mum breezed into my room, humming. The talking stopped. That was much better. Her wispy, gliding frame was all that blocked the light as she began to open my curtains.

"Hey! Leave them shut!" I protested. She gasped at how rough I looked and said I could stay off school. The winner was that I'd miss all those boring lessons. But no way could I do my dance class, with all that running to the loo stuff still going on.

I had a nice lie-in, though. When Mum realised I was burning up, she gave me paracetamol. "You OK? Why not try something to eat?" she went. I rolled over; I was barely able to lift my head off the pillow, never mind eat. She draped a wet flannel over my forehead, freezing me. Then she went to take a brush to my unravelled brown plaits.

"Really, Mum?" I murmured. I was out of it until the middle of the afternoon, when Dad came up pacing and he woke me. I felt them standing over me, praying, and that made me jump. Boiling sunlight still blasted in.

Mum felt my head. "Arhhh! It hurts!" That scared her. My head was thumping; everything looked blurry. The high temperature was taking me on some dodgy, out-of-body trip.

Mum panicked, "This isn't right. Her temperature's exploding. Should her eyes look like that?" Her voice was too high-pitched.

Dad shook his head. "No!" he croaked. "She looks flushed but what more can I do?" The rustling sound of the pages of his sacred book deafened me. My senses were extreme; I was gagging for iced water.

"Drink," I said but they couldn't make me out. Suddenly the deafening noise stopped. The pain stopped and I felt better. I had the surreal sensation of floating up, in slow motion. I looked down from the ceiling of the Manse (that's the name of our weird house). My face went red and blotchy. Everything was well strange.

Mum was shocked. "Tal, what's happening?"

As if I knew.

She noticed my hair was manky. "This is more than a normal fever!" Dad's thickset frame should have made me feel even hotter as he knelt so close I caught his breath. But I didn't need it. Dad's chants were intense directly from the text.

Mum just kept mumbling: "Talitha, Talitha!" Then she burst into tears, quivering uncontrollably, and shook me. After zero response from me, she bit her lip. "She's limp!" she shrieked at my poor dad; this time she collapsed.

He sat her down to kiss Mum's shaking head. "I'm getting help. We need Dr J. I'm off down to the beach." My cousin Pete followed him; same old thing. Like a dork with his puny shadow. Annoyingly, with the older cousin always allowed to do the fun bits, I wasn't surprised the boy had kept out of my dramatics until then.

"The doctor's coming," Mum repeated down the phone. He would sort me out. Or could he? Shame about all the bad things I'd ever done whirled through my brain. But my thoughts were interrupted by screams and panic. "It's too late!"

Sheila, our nice neighbour came in. "She can't be gone... I don't believe it. We must be able to do something."

Mum saw my relaxed face, as if I'd dropped off. "Talitha, don't go!" She sounded so desperate. My cruising around the ceiling was interrupted. I watched my body being worked over and breaths being forced into me. Mum and Sheila refused to give up. Bless them.

My heart stopped. "She's slipping away!" Sheila continued rattling my frame with chest compressions whilst Mum gave breaths until she was exhausted. It looked terrifying.

Mum collapsed back onto the brown, woven rug by my bed. "What next?" With me giving off over-and-out signs, it seemed ages until Dr J. made his epic entrance. Dad had also brought three faith soothers with him and noisily ushered them into my room, then rushed over to Mum. She was losing it big time, ripping up her scarf fringe into pieces and wailing that I was too young to die. He held her hand.

It was kind of fascinating seeing me from this angle. I only ever saw myself in a mirror, with my eyes open. Now I could see what I looked like when I was asleep; I could see myself as others saw me. That was weird. Although I was kind of enjoying this, I wanted to get back down there; to look out again, rather than in. I hated seeing my parents so upset.

Then Dr J., dressed in his coolest blue shorts, hugged my mum calmly. "Why are you crying?" he asked as if there was no emergency. His curly, almost shoulder-length hair was windswept. I could smell the sea spray waft in on it. His dark, warm eyes examined me.

"Our daughter's dead," Dad explained, sounding wounded.

Dr J. turned slowly from my shell. "No, she's only sleeping."

It was terrible because I had no voice when I just wanted to shout out that he was correct. Then, he took hold of my hand and told me to get up. That's when I shot back into my body and I was normal once more. His firm touch left a bizarre tingling sensation. Bring it on! "I owe you big time," I squeaked inside my head.

"My love, you're back!" Mum cried.

Dad grinned. "Tal, thank God. You're alive!"

"I'm alright, really. You're the man, Dr J. I'm mended. I think!" I laughed. A gasp went around my bedroom.

"Thanks, you're a life saver," I said.

"That's good," he said, rubbing my head.

My parents humbly repeated, "Thank you," shaking his hand.

"You must stay for dinner," Dad requested.

"Feed your hungry daughter first. Enjoy! Sorry, we'll have to pass," replied Dr J.

His mate warned everyone to keep quiet over what had just happened. "This mustn't get out or everyone will want a bit of him." Dad nodded. "Please, just remember him privately," said the soother before the procession left. They made out like we must forget a miracle ever happened…

And there began my overprotection party.[5]

---

[5] This is a modern-day retelling of the bible story of Jairus's daughter.

Paradise Lost... Not!

IT'S THE SAME PLACE BUT YOU'D HARDLY RECOGnise it. This time, the second time, it's very different! Better, that is. There's a new order. We have claimed our inheritance. I absorb the rays and feel the warmth that's energised me. Flawless is the word that explains most things here. And there's joy beyond my smile. Fulfilment oozes from my pores. It's awesome!

This free passage was promised to everyone. Only, no one knew when it would come, or where it would come from. It just happened to come when we, Jack and Sue, were on the other side of the world. We were in deepest Asia, enjoying a special holiday. This wonderful event kicked off on the day we had planned to meet the staff at the orphanage that our church sponsored. This holiday might last forever, though. My concern was that all my family weren't here too; it was just our youngest, Fran, and her mate, Kate.

This didn't suit some. By that I mean those who couldn't believe in a free lunch, never mind free passage. Just like it was at home. We were in unfamiliar territory. I expected it to be hot but not this hot! This was stifling. That was because an erupting volcano was steaming in front of our four-wheeled vehicle. The island was in danger of being engulfed. We didn't realise it had been inactive for years. The tour rep (a native of the island) panicked when the dust began to choke us. He turned the Land Rover around, and expected us to go with him. His instructions were translated through headphones, but we knew we were being fed lies. He was not the one to trust. Luckily for us, we'd brought our own tried and tested guide. He directed us, and we followed; the four of us went to face the last challenge.

Paradise Lost... Not!

"Oh, no!" I gasped, as I saw the distinctive red glow spread over the vehicle. Droplets from the encroaching wave of lava were falling on it. A group of doubting locals insisted on making their own separate way. They were led by the fool; it was such a shame. I tried to show them another way, a safe passage. I invited them to follow us. "Come with me, please!" I pleaded. But what could I do? My husband tried, too. They'd heard it before, but the pull of the old world was too strong.

"Who are you to say you've got the answers?" one said cynically. They'd been betrayed by blind ignorance and all its shortcomings. The media had seduced them with false promises of third-world wealth. If only they understood that wealth didn't equal contentment. But they were reluctant to let go of these lies. The same false props kept many at home in chains. And still the manipulative demon raged, giving false hope of an instant high. He had the cheek to say it was what they deserved. I'd tried to remove the blinkers from several of them, but now their fallout was eternal. Unfortunately, their addictions were lethal! They often mocked us when we tried to show them the right way. That made me sick with fear. It was as if we spoke a different language.

Still, each soul was worth the effort. But time was ticking by, and our last call went out. "We must follow this wise man," said Jack, as he pointed up ahead. He was desperately trying to persuade the stragglers. Our friend was athletic, a true forerunner. We took him at his word.

"This way to the tree of life," he declared. I breathed a sigh of relief at the reassurance of our guide, but some gasped in terror. They realised that their clock had stopped, that their purpose had been spent. For these poor souls, there was no way back. They randomly bolted, pushing and shoving one another. Their faces were grey from shock. They were stumbling but still striving.

I heard our guide ahead shout. "Stop! For God's sake, STOP!" But they didn't hear. They were moving farther away, but in the wrong direction. It was tragic. They were like rabbits caught in the headlights, and they just ran towards the heat. Complicated reasons were preventing them from simply stopping and turning away. They remained blinkered by the drivel that had previously seemed important in their quest to be individuals.

"To join is to gain. Please say you're sorry and accept I'm the one to lead you safely home." His was such a simple message, but 'united we stand' was never their motto. We couldn't stop these few slipping into the path of fiery disaster. There was a scorched line where the foul magma cooled. It oozed from the fiery centre, reaching to the surface of the earth. Crackling flames enveloped the defiant, dragging the last of them back, screeching. I covered my ears. They left claw marks, etched forever in the ground, a terrible reminder of this time. I wondered if a memorial would be built here in the days ahead. When I covered my eyes to ease the anticipated smoke-induced soreness, I realised they were fine. Our battle had ended when a deafening burst of relief-gas escaped from the awesome volcano's chimney. It blew our small group up to the safety of higher ground. The soil had majestically cooled. Relieved, we bowed down, chanting thanks, as our knees buckled.

"Hooray!" everyone shouted. We began to enter a lovely cooling tunnel, full of wafts of sweet mercy. We glided along in it. Next to it was a bottomless box, into which I was happy to drop my baggage; this was marked *Forgotten*. On the far side was a shoot marked *Restored*. That's where we emerged, surrounded by children.

Paradise Lost... Not!

I spoke with a woman who was corralling them like lambs. "You must be from the Rosie Orphanage. Please tell me I'm right. We were on our way to see you."

She nodded. "Thank you so much. Yes, this is us." Sheer relief washed over us both as we welcomed them. More joiners! Great! I'd taken a girl in each hand by now, big as they were. But then my husband faltered. I looked back at him. "What's up, Dad?" I heard Fran ask him.

"Your brother and sister from back home? Tell me when you spot them. We must all look out for them." That went without saying.

"Of course we will, Dad. Sure. They'll be here somewhere."

I glanced at Kate, who told me that she was worried about some of her family. I gave her a hug. She couldn't go back for them; it was just too dangerous. The gnashing flames hadn't melted us but to go back would be treacherous. A wall of clear water marked a charcoaled line of protection across the land. We were glad of that. "Who would have thought that the tears of the lost and defiant, lapping around our feet, would save us?" I had blurted it out loud. The mighty power of water rose up to calm the bubbling, red-hot explosion. The aggressor was finally quietened. We feared the worst but found we were in for a treat. Then all the rubbish had been erased from my memory. We moved on.

There was plenty to look forward to. As rubber-neckers at the greatest act of God, we were amazed to see the scales dangling in front of us. The scales were lowered from the high canopy, secured on each side by strong twisted bark. These carefully weighed the truth in each soul. Through the smoke-filled clouds it was difficult to make out the judge. But the vines connected the all-seeing branches of the ancient forest, which was marked with a crown. The judge found us in his book, ticked off our names, and we were allowed up. We were relieved to find our other daughter and son had made it. We found them safe with our gran. Dad grabbed them. "Well done for doing as we did," he said. Jo and Liz completed our family triumph. We now had eternity in which to catch up with them. As promised, our flock were regrouping as conscripts under the new law. Huge sprawling branches were directing the flow beyond human traffic. It was an absolute picture: the generations reuniting. When Jack caught up with his dad they fell into a man hug, vowing never again to let go of one another. Grandpa Tom came over to them. "I knew you'd make it, son." They spent hours catching up. You could sense that the pressure was off; they just chilled.

It felt like it was Christmas here. Savouring this, I pressed on with the songbird as my guide. Fortunately, the cool wind blew sense through us; we knew we had been created for a purpose. Recognising the absolute freedom in our familiar guide's eyes, I was glad I had chosen to spend time with him. And then I heard a whisper: "It's finished, your job's been done well." It came from where the judge and guide sat. Each creature had its say, restored because of its blameless ways. A couple of pure white doves swooped overhead, near the eagle that had taken the top perch. The very old and the confused were totally restored. It was fantastic to witness the release of a new order. There was so much to take in. We each received a regal handshake. That marked the beginning of the Second Coming.

My eyes latched onto Jack. His face shone back at me. "Sue, I told you so," he mouthed. He stepped forward to give me a kiss. My ears tuned into the choir and the awesome orchestra that was playing us into the new universe. An incredible brightness took over. Such happiness! Everyone already knew where I'd come from and they didn't judge me. My cleansing was completed by a warm shower that washed away any remaining stains. I'd come through a process where my self-esteem had been gathered up. There were no more puzzles in this life. I'd been helped by my loved ones, who had also picked themselves up, dusted themselves off and started over. We decided that all things were possible. Here there was no room for failure. We were all winners because the battle had been fought for us. I accepted this place as a refuge where every member of my family could achieve full potential. I experienced a terrific lightness, signifying sheer joy. I looked around, delighted to see there were more of us than I could have dreamed of, and without even so much as one of our toes being burnt! That was such a relief.

"This place has been tugging on my soul since forever," a fresh voice sang. When I splashed water on my face in a pool, I noticed that my reflection wasn't the familiar one. I didn't panic, though, because I knew that it was still me. I looked over at Kate and Fran. They had changed, of course; they were even more beautiful. Yet we were uniquely connected by our past. The Perfect One reigned over this place, and threw a fantastic welcoming party. His son sat next to him. He was our guide. He offered words that I treasured, words about me belonging here. Those reassuring words felt hugely comforting. Although his appearance was new, his love had been constant. He was wiser and more awesome than I had dared imagine.

Our language was reminiscent of the old memory verses. The words tripping off the tongue of our dear friend Jacob provided absolute proof that we were in the intended place. It was my time to relax and reap the benefits of all my trials.

Promises I had counted on had come good. They'd taught me so much. I was grateful that we were with our whole family. What was all too evident now was that they were no longer our children. They were no longer our responsibility because their allotted time had come.

I was sometimes surprised to meet the newbies. Many brave souls were repaid for doing fine things, sometimes secretly. How generous was the Perfect One! It was beyond what we deserved. The words *Freedom Reigns* had been written across the sky by swooping swifts. And then I noticed that I was moving freely, and I skipped along. "My pain's all gone!" I shouted.

My daughters giggled at me, inviting me to join them in their jive. My struggles had dissolved into the rainbow of the new vivid colours of the victory flag that was streaming above. I feared nothing. I looked upon my husband's face and saw that the lines that had been etched through concern and hard work had been smoothed away. We could relax and be glad. He held my hand and asked me to dance. This was a miracle in its own right. Old ailments from years ago had stolen moments like this. All our work had been completed and the real prize had been won.

The little children played safely, and no longer hassled their parents for their next meal. That was thanks to a bountiful supply of easily picked fruits and adequate spring water. They played hide and seek in the luscious tropical paradise. They squealed at the challenge of catching the seeds that blew on the breeze like floating playthings. It was pleasantly warm and the blooms were sprinkled with light showers at night. Fuchsias and sweet peas grew like weeds, giving a constant splash of pinks, purples and reds. These cheerful blossoms exuded a seductive scent. Everything was new and life was easy. At last we accepted that we were safe.

Paradise Lost... Not!

The country was now in perfect balance. This was definitely the place to be. Great gifts that had been promised long ago now lined our path. Each of us had rooms prepared for us; there was plenty for everyone. There was no more disappointment, only fun. My friends were always cooking up healthy lashings of encouragement, dished out with each tasty meal. I regularly collapsed in my hammock and let it rock gently, without a worry. There was nowhere else I was meant to be. I was full of all I needed and my loved ones were all around me. There were no more tears. It seemed we'd hit the jackpot.

All the inhabitants had been engrained with the contentment that ran through the middle of this land. Complete joy was absorbed with each sip of the clean water. We were resting under the shadow of not only our guide but also the Perfect One, who sat on glistening seats at the head of a never-ending buffet table! This was a win-win situation. We felt like honoured guests of the bride, being on the top table. Everyone was included in these celebrations. We raised our glasses and I turned to Jack: "It's an absolute miracle to end up in Paradise!"[6]

---

[6] Included in *The Heavenly Road Trip* eBook with Help for Writers, 2012

Meg's Diary

DON'T ASK ME HOW I EVER ENDED UP HERE. THE last thing I can remember was an air raid siren going off! What I do know is that I'm sick and tired of running. So, where are your mates when you need them? "Chris, Steve, where are you?" I bellow but not a murmur of a reply comes back. The ground's been rumbling for days. There's been looting and worse, so much worse! Roughed up people are wandering around looking for their families. It's total confusion. Even this place I once knew well is remote. All I do know is I managed to get on this smooth escalator; then I stumbled across this incredible leatherbound diary. *A load of rubbish* was my first thought but then I was so tired I fell asleep, slumped over it. Unreal, I relaxed for the first time in ages. My raw eyes refused to stay prised apart a moment longer.

But when I woke up with a jerk a full two hours later, the diary had closed and I noticed her photo, pasted on the back. It was Meg, this beautiful blonde with magnificent blue eyes. Suddenly, I was alone with only what I lay down in. It was my gut feeling that I was safe, for the time being. So I just continued reading.

MEG'S DIARY – Dare to look!!

The final week ... Ignoring this message may seriously damage your health.

Day 1

Be careful! By now you're in terrible danger. Please, don't let this be the last thing you ever read!

Meg's Diary

Still, I feel sad for you. I'm safe. When you are ready to join me, follow. I don't know you, so I'll call you Seeker. Now, I'll try to tell it like it is.

<u>*Day 2*</u>

Think about it. My story is that I'm just a no one. I'm a no one called Meg who's waiting for you, Seeker. I'll try to put you in the picture. Up until the last few weeks my life has been uneventful. I'm a normal 16-year-old, but I see now that it's how I've lived that's really mattered. There are consequences to our actions. Don't blame yourself, though, you weren't to know; hardly anyone does from the West. It's harder the older you are. I'm from a colony long forgotten. My life changed big time at my grandma's reckoning service. That's when I got this extreme message.

<u>*Day 3*</u>

Understand me. From here on there is no way back. By now you'll have come up the escalator, halfway to the station (it speeds up). Next, you'll notice a pair of pure white doves who'll guide you to the sorting booth. You'll go on the scales where your time and future are balanced... I know it's hard to grasp but our Leader's Son will then consider you whilst you take a long look in the mirror. He's awesome and fair. He's on the other side, watching. If he finds you on his list, you'll come the right way and join us in Forevermore. I beg you to let your heart lead your soul. Then your body and mind will be renewed, your identity redefined. It's great. Through our Leader your heart will be satisfied. I promise you, I tell you

41

the truth that in Forevermore you will be made complete. All becomes clear here, when you join.

Day 4

Beware. The alternative is ruin, worse than you could imagine. A complete nightmare! Don't be tempted to try going down in the shadows like those blinkered proud people and get sucked in the foul deafening black hole! Away from the station is off limits. Keep on coming. Please, don't lose hope. Stop the Trickster, a liar, into conning you to consider yourself unworthy of entering. You're welcome to join us when you're ready. It's a natural progression. This reckoning time comes to us all.

Day 5

To be rich is to need the least. Seeker, I pray it becomes clear. Logical and right. I've been given something precious, real hope. Our Leader's son earned us that, free passage to Forevermore. Where I'm from we're used to having little. We rated it all, each other and the law. I was taught to keep short accounts. I'd learnt to treat others better than me. It's been easy for me; being poor we just had to share and help each other out or we wouldn't have survived. We had respect and fear anyhow; I'm used to serving. Yet those with too much have more to surrender. We all need to. It's tough but keep on going.

Day 6

Persevere. The only way to find out is to believe and trust. I really hope that your family have preceded you here and chosen this way to see the new dawn. Don't presume all of my family made it. Here, you'll

Meg's Diary

find complete peace because pain plays no part. It's a brand-new kingdom where all treasures are waiting for us to enjoy. So what's keeping you?

<u>*The Last Day - 7*</u>

Join me. Read off the card, on your knees, if you want to say you're sorry. Or you could even sing it in your heart. I hope it's all familiar, this renewing of your vows. There're no mistakes; if you've been robbed of your talents and dreams, it's time to recapture them. Let me tell you, the price has been paid for us all. This is the time; please think carefully. Many are on the wrong path; believe and trust the Son. I beg you, Seeker.

Heavy! I did feel a bit better when I came across our Steve. We just clung to each other. I was thinking that I should tell him... I held Meg's picture close, guarding her from Steve's prying eyes.

"Give us a gander at your precious book, will you, Rob?"

"Lay off, mind your own business!" I snapped back. Having got a glimpse of someone out there who cared, I didn't want to let her go. Surprisingly, I really missed my folks even after all their moaning and my running away; I actually missed their nagging! It made me wonder whether they really had loved me. The sharp stomach pain reminded me of my absolute hunger. I couldn't think straight. There I was, going up this escalator, not knowing when it would stop, but then the station was coming up ahead.

But then it dawned on me. "Steve, come on mate, we need to just keep going. There's a girl up here reckons she's got all the answers." I was still wondering what day I was on.

But Steve wouldn't listen. "What? You must be mad; it looks far more fun this way." And he was gone.

"Catch you later," I called after him. But I was back on my own – or was I? Moving the diary from under my arm, a loose sheet fell to the ground.

In fancy gilt lettering it read in thankfulness for the life of Mrs. Peggy Swain:

Remember your Creator in the days of your youth,
Before the days of trouble come and the years approach when you will say,
I find no pleasure in them – before the sun and the light
And the moon and the stars grow dark, and the clouds return after the rain.
When men rise up at the sound of birds, but all their songs grow faint,
When men are afraid of heights and of the dangers in the streets.
When the almond tree blossoms and the grasshopper drags himself along
And desire no longer is stirred.
Then man goes to his eternal home and mourners go about the streets.
Remember him – before the silver cord is severed, or the golden bowl is broken;
Before the pitcher is shattered at the spring, or the wheel broken at the well.
And the dust returns to the ground it came from,
And the spirit returns to God who gave it.

Meg's Diary

I gulped because I knew it was for Meg's gran. Could she really be trying to help me, even when my parents didn't think I deserved a second chance? I'd love to believe this tale Meg had left me. A huge consideration! I'd love to dare to dream of happiness, freedom and plenty. All I needed? I wish! Hanging my head low, I pulled up my hood. My mind was full of regret. I shut my eyes, wiping them on my sleeve.

Only, to my surprise came a gentle whisper of, "It's time." Then a purple light shone, giving off this lovely waft of warm scented breeze...[7]

---

[7] Included in *The Heavenly Road Trip* eBook with Help for Writers, 2012

Finding Myself as the Tide Turns

GROWING UP, I TOOK A COW AND CALF ROCKS playground for granted. This forever home was in my grandma's purple gorse backyard. For starters, I only visited for the summer. No wonder I doodled in exercise book margins when the scenery revealed classic, rugged landscape. Looking out from my bedroom window kind of helped my awkward family situation disappear. So, I happily stayed. Hannah stopped me adding "Sarah was ere" to local boulders because she belonged there. My BFF came from a close family. Lucky her!

As a newbie, I did these cool charcoal rubbings of ancient carvings near St Margaret's church with Miss at Primary. Going outdoors was the main attraction then. That teacher recognising my sketching potential began an infatuation for patterns. Anyone noticing me was on to a complete winner. As curiosity grew to discover art carved on natural stone landmarks, I emulated those patterns in local drawings. Thus, I survived by bringing smiles to the faces of people who counted me in. Such revelations came to a teenager, jogging around this wild backyard with a friend. More recently, I traced the carved grooves in weathered sandstone with my fingertips. They showed loved-up couples' names within hearts. It was more like graffiti, but still actual proof of their family history. Unsurprisingly, my parents' tag was missing. Then it was too late for me to add to the rock because that would be faking it. Who needed a dad anyway?

Before, I tried to sidetrack Gran asking, "Have you heard of the goddess Verbeia?" This was after learning about traditional cults which often left their mark in the wild, prompting my obsession in folklore. But Gran rejected the

Finding Myself as the Tide Turns

Romano-Celtic divinity associated with our local Ilkley and the nearby River Wharfe, which I researched. She took those reference books straight back to the library.

My grandma soon put me straight with, "No! And don't bother telling me because I'm not interested in such fantasy. Sarah, you do know I am totally interested in you, though!" She stared inquisitively as if I were still six years old and just recently landed on her doorstep. My cheeks burnt to realise a healthy reverence for the beautiful, inspiring landscape was not what Gran worried about. It was more the threat of my running away to join a cult that gave her the heebie-jeebies. Understandably, she wanted to avoid history repeating itself. All this nonsense equalled me being booked on a religious retreat in Lindisfarne.

Gran threatened me with that mini-break for my seventeenth birthday. She insisted that her God was the real one; not the pagan type worshipped years ago at Bolton Abbey. I suppose she just wanted me safe so when my experimentation with permanent body-art tipped her into panic mode, she freaked out. On spotting my innocent butterfly tattoo that fluttered above my wrist after a seaside trip with Hannah, Gran worried body sculpture could become my latest craze. At the time, belonging was a real issue for me. It might have had something to do with her refusal to explain why Mum ignored me for eleven years. Whatever! She cared. I loved her because she couldn't bear to lose me, as well. *No more uprooting of our family tree* was her motto.

Planning ahead, Gran insisted I find her God alive in Lindisfarne country. She hoped by tuning me into this believing zone, I might forgive my mum for abandoning me. "It's time to grow up, Sarah!" she said. While I was dragged to church before, this growing up phase was far scarier. But,

47

if University was ever to be on the horizon, then she must trust my instincts. Google reassured me about the trip when I read, "The body can be fortified with Lindisfarne Mead." That was the preferred holy spirit there.

"Go on, then, if I have to," I caved in. At least the drinking part was my kind of healing. Having conquered getting lost jogging in fog on the Moors, an east coast escape for a free holiday sounded doable.

When Hannah found out about my punishment, she said, "That will teach you to play the geek. Man-up, Sarah, it will hardly kill you!"

"Shut up! It is what it is. I'll cope." I got a grip. But as the weekend arrived, I faked the flu to avoid going. Gran wasn't falling for that though. Bizarrely, after a boring bus trip, I crossed the causeway onto a pretty island that eerily slipped into the sea. Spying the 'idiot hut' from the window, for those who got caught out by the tide, intrigued me. On arrival, acting posh wasn't easy as other retreat guests were mostly seniors. Meaning, once introductions were done, I lost my confidence and legged-it. They say that old habits die hard. It was down to feelings of uselessness.

"Why are we all here?" was the innocent trigger from our retreat leader. Apparently, that was a perfectly reasonable question to his attentive, tea-drinking circle. But I panicked, pushing the seat back and bolting. Disappearing off outside didn't leave the best first impression on the group. A seagull screeched 'like mother, like daughter' accusations flying down towards the sea. I simply had to chase him off.

That question isn't for me; I should have passed. James knew I needed to get my head together to consider getting a decent education. Why ask complicated questions at the

Finding Myself as the Tide Turns

start? He asked for trouble when I had no room in my life for any more aggravation.

Their whole trial independence concept gave me palpitations. Stress was not what I'd anticipated from this weekend away, but tripping up the street past the tearoom led to a narrow footpath and safely onto the beach. I got my breath back. My attention switched to a random woman hobbling along ahead. A salty breeze persuaded me to scrape my wispy ginger curls back tightly into a ponytail. Alone there, I could push tides of embarrassment away. Instinctively, I noticed that strange woman had kicked off her shiny black shoes. The trace of invading waves left crazy paving bubbles on them. But where was she? She couldn't have gone into the sea fully dressed, surely. Nervously, I gulped as if needing permission to haul the footwear back to shore, checking that no one watched as I realigned them.

Waiting, as my feet sank into the tiny shells on the shore, I almost missed nature's treat of a shoal of silvery tiddlers swimming by. Together, we rippled the surface of the sea, forming our temporary peaceful spot. Only when the ghostly seal pups stopped barking from behind the rocky outcrop, I de-stressed by following on into the lapping waves up to my knees. Worrying that she was an attention-seeker made my mouth dry. Coming ashore to steady myself against a bench, I gulped in the crisp air. Giving my throat a gentle rub, I soaked in the historic surroundings and tried to get a grip while the sun dried my skin. Shutting my eyes helped clear my thoughts of tricks. *All this must be in your head, Sarah.* Backing off, rushing inland, I shouted, "But I never asked to be born!" My pitiful cry echoed through the brick archway. Glancing downwards, a plaque read how years ago the Norman Priory ruin was robbed of its stone by Henry VIII to build Lindisfarne Castle. Hiding under this ruin's shadow,

I appreciated other epic testimonies written about some significant families now anchored on ancient flagstones.

A tearful blink treasured a fading mirage of the woman's familiar frame melting into that Friday evening. Beyond the crumbling mortar, underneath the moonlight, her outline was scrubbed out. After rubbing my eyes, I shook. It was the point of realising many had fallen apart in this spiritual haven. The robbed monks must have been frantic at King Henry's ferocious attack! An empathy with past, poor souls shouldn't have made me feel better. However, it somehow did. As the real and unreal merged over an endless, flaming skyline, anything seemed possible. A stab of adrenalin shot up my spine propelling me back towards the retreat. Once in the house, I slunk amongst the gathering where I pulled an inhaler from my backpack. Red-faced, I denied giving them eye-contact. Tiptoeing, grabbing a bottle of water off the sideboard, I slid on my chair. Spotting the ceramic butterfly on the wall excited my creative mojo. Drawing a perfect symmetrical red admiral proved challenging. By concentrating on sketching delicate wings, half-listening helped to anaesthetise my current hijacked state.

James asked, "Why do you think Jesus loves each and every one of us?" His cringeworthy efforts at helping us to find hope gave him some kind of street credibility. I felt ashamed I'd chased the ghost of my mum away, as James merrily chatted to the converted participants. Glancing around the conservatory, the leaded lights from the colourful window panes projected the sun's setting rays across their faces. Happily wearing our halos, us guests sought true restoration.

"That means we all must have plus-ones now," a spinster joked, scanning the room for approval. James was quick to enthuse about real bible promises making each of us worthy

Finding Myself as the Tide Turns

of receiving love. Basking in undeserved glory, we crunched jammy dodgers relieved to have arrived. My breathing had barely calmed down before he extended my comfort zone further, though. Maybe James forgot his brief was, "Come to me, all who are weary." Plainly, he should avoid poking us until we squirm. A tingling spasm shot up my spine. Sadly, there was no alcoholic stimulus to dull our senses, only stuff of the Spirit! What tough luck; to misunderstand the trip's bonus.

Thus, the final declaration of, "Because Christ died and rose again for all to have eternal life," from a dog-collared, greying participant was welcomed by approving nods. James grinned at his star pupil. Clueless about giving any similar angelic response, my shoulders hunched as the conversation snake slithered my way. I couldn't spit out a croaky whimper, even a swig of water was too much effort. Being paralysed, staring up hopeful of a miracle was all I could do. Then sliding back into my seat, deep sobs allowed my disappointments to escape. Letting go of such sadness helped me forget about my mum. Thinking, *Gran will always protect me. And at University, God will keep me going.*

Back in the room, a nod from James towards a box of tissues indulged a vulnerable adult like me. I rated his inclusivity. Then, he pushed our personal responsibility boundaries to encourage taking hold of the faith. This was his awkward point: "It implies we are equipped to come through our trials. How do you think that can happen?"

A neighbour on the table embraced the gift: "Of course, Jesus left the Holy Spirit to empower us..." There, I languished in her success. Her head-scratching made me nervous, so I finished the sentence for her.

I blurted out, "By us attempting to do what God wants us to do, from reading the bible." Cheating in interpreting the purple, wall-mounted tapestry scripture, "But we understand these things, for we have the mind of Christ." Those smart embroidered words hung in a speech bubble, coming from a smiley mouth. To merge into the background, I copied the curly, golden shape on my jotter's new page thinking, *Will that include me? Can I ever be strong enough?* It was rubbish acting like an imposter looking in on life. Recently, I wanted to have confidence.

I sighed, accepting God had chosen me despite my dodgy ancestry. On that Sunday, wading through the saltwater over to the neighbouring St Cuthbert's Island dot, I discovered Psalm 93:4 posted on a rock. My lightbulb moment was confirmed. "Mightier than the thunders of many waters, mightier than the waves of the sea, the Lord on high is mighty!" I thought, *even Gran would approve of this graffiti.* When I said sorry, then it ditched my past history and was such a sheer release. The ancient place enabled me to bury memories deep into the sand to become free.

Returning home the same evening, Gran smiled as she noticed how chilled I appeared. The following day Hannah and I giggled looking at cute, creased baby photos of me with my parents. Their perplexed faces, studied so often, looked kinder since I found myself. Also, I admitted to my friend, the Moor's pictures were dodgy to infer water collected in cups as a magic cure for all ailments. Also, by emulating the cult artwork, I'd tried to fix myself. From this time onwards, I wanted what prayer could offer. Looking back was a waste of energy. Trusting in the love of God was the key to future happiness. The whole scribbling phase made me passionate about something, at least.

Wide-eyed, Hannah said, "I think I get you, Sarah!" She gave a thumbs-up to my using both mind and heart to rate

Finding Myself as the Tide Turns

significant issues. Lately, on our runs, my mate let me jog ahead without fear of me doing something stupid. Apparently, trust was a two-way thing.

At last Sunday's service, Gran confirmed that pagan relics' messages weren't exactly healthy. She was delighted with my clean slate and reassured God would fill the gap in my heart. Seeing how hard it was to get my head around a past all-forgiven, Gran declared, "Tomorrow is another day, Sarah!" That was nice. Finally, we agreed on something.

The tide turned on my future the moment I felt qualified to be loved. For a short while longer, I safely belonged in my gran's landscape. My University application was more confident from several recent, enthusiastic edits. It seemed my life was getting sorted out since I had a new purpose. At University, I'd have time to explore belief further and gain lifelong friends. I figured that all meant I was good enough.

So whatever tomorrow brings, it will be fine to just be me.

The Blessings of Cotgrave Colliery in Our Back Yard

DURING 1953-54 WITH THE DISCOVERY OF COAL around Cotgrave in South Nottinghamshire, there came plans for a colliery. Cotgrave Colliery's short life wasn't so cutting edge for our farming family as for the miners, but similarly enforced diversification upon them. When my husband's parents first cleared a wood to make a smallholding at Stragglethorpe, near Cotgrave, little did they know of the changes that the colliery would bring to their day-to-day. Since 1946, at Thornton's Holt, my parents-in-law worked a small farm with a few acres of potatoes, pigs, goats and hens. Serendipitously, a French hole-boring company sent workers to camp on their field in the 1950s and thus initiated the gradual change of use of their farmland. That switch in business was to a seasonal campsite during the warmer months, alongside their production and sale of free-range eggs, chickens, potatoes and salad crops from the greenhouse. This sale of farm produce was carried out at the gate and then later at an on-site camp shop. My mother-in-law, father-in-law and husband became quite the entrepreneurs. My husband was the youngest of their three boys, called Will.

The building of a two-and-three-quarter-mile branch mineral line diverging from the Nottingham-Grantham railway line preceded the colliery opening. That extended from Nottingham past Radcliffe-on-Trent to cut through my father-in-law's main field to service the colliery. So, this mineral railway line cut straight through one of their fields in 1960, rendering their land use options reduced. The mine

The Blessings of Cotgrave Colliery in Our Back Yard

didn't open for a couple more years. The benefit to our family was a small monetary compensation alongside a fresh opportunity for making a living. Although this local development was considered a mixed blessing at the time, as the change came at the cost of a small Jersey herd of milkers, the cows sadly had to be taken to market because there was no longer sufficient grazing land to feed them. Farming life was predictable until the Jersey cows left.

So, my husband's parents stepped cautiously into the unknown, enjoying playing host to the French workers camping next to their home for minimal reward. The distinctive thing about Cotgrave colliery was that the koepe towers at the pit head were considered very modern compared with other pit head winding gear towers. Also, face workers benefited from modern changing rooms and showers. Coal taken from Cotgrave was taken by train to Ratcliffe on Trent power station to fuel the generation of electricity for a large proportion of the East Midlands.

There was much anticipation of improved prosperity in the small village of Cotgrave. Then, we experienced some cultural diversity as our new best mates from school often talked with unfamiliar Geordie accents. Will and I were in our teens so had not yet met. I loved to hear them sing their sentences. There was an influx of five hundred experienced mine workers and their families from the North East who accepted National Coal Board tied houses, complete with furniture. With that influx of miners, the population of Cotgrave gradually went from a mere 700 to 5,000. They occupied a purpose-built housing estate in the village. That meant improved services and a shopping precinct for us all to enjoy. Members of many local families increased their household income by having a son train to go down the pit. My husband and I met several new friends at senior school from the North East. I remember one exciting school trip to visit the pit head to witness the coal-dusted men come up in a cage. That gave me a new respect for their dirty and sometimes dangerous occupation.

Sadly, the east-facing railway chord shut in 1976 having been last used three years earlier. As a young person, Will welcomed the interruption of coal trains enjoying running alongside in an attempt to beat the train. Occasionally, the driver threw him lumps of coal for their fire. Quiet excitement came in 1977, when for the Jubilee celebrations, the queen stayed overnight at Stragglethorpe on the mineral line, in her Majesty's Royal train. Our family respected Her Majesty's privacy, noticing her Royal Protection Team in a car under the railway bridge.

During early 1993 the National Union of Mineworkers marched in opposition to the closure. Shockingly for the local community, in 1993-94 the Cotgrave mine shut due to the millions of tonnes of seams reserved being of poor quality. That coal for fuelling the power station was no longer affordable. Subterranean streams and subsequent flooding, along with the growing remoteness of the coal face from the shaft drastically increased the cost of bringing the coal to the surface. Eventually, the railway line morphed into a foot/cycle path courtesy of Nottinghamshire County Council. The shafts were filled with concrete on closure and all associated buildings demolished.

There is now a Cotgrave Country Park and new housing on the old site. So Cotgrave Colliery is gone but not forgotten by the Linday family and many others besides.[8]

---

[8] Included in *An East Midlands Coalmining Anthology* by Natalie Braber & David Amos; Five Leaves Books; autumn 2021

Lord, My King and My God

Lord, my king and my God, I pray to you.
Lord, my king and my God, I pray to you.
As you listen to honesty, I wait.
So you know I'm grateful, truly grateful.

Please let me daily turn your way.
Expecting you clearly hear my voice,
I'm glad that you listen when I pray.

Crying out for more help, I pray to you.
Crying out for more help, I pray to you.
As you take on my laments, I stay.
So you know I'm grateful, truly grateful.

Please let me bow down in safety.
With such pure love you wish me changed;
I'm glad you direct my steps greatly.

Needing some of your hope, I work for you.
Needing some of your hope, I work for you.
As you share in my laments, I sing.
So you know I'm grateful, truly grateful.

Then, please let us try doing right.
As you protect us with a caring shield,
We're so glad to have you in the fight.

Lord, my King and my God, we pray to you.
Lord, my King and my God, we pray to you.
As you collect our praises, we celebrate.

Count Our Blessings

So you know we're grateful, truly grateful.

Then, please let us show all your joy.
As you long for all our praises and worship,
We're glad making sounds that you enjoy.[9]

---

[9] This song was sparked from the *Singing with Joy Through Life* training at Cornerstone Church, Nottingham.

The Real Me

MY MUM WASN'T ALWAYS A COMEDIAN. LATELY, though, her nerves are rubbish. While I can't catch her upsetting ways, the idea of my losing the plot consumes me. My dad's last piece of advice was, "Live each day to the full because life's not a rehearsal." Since then I pack in the fun. But she misses him, and it triggers her profanity, making things impossible. Such a sad history cramps my style, and I need to take care of what I wish for. Somehow, I'll work out how to honour his wishes.

Until, 'on stage' at the surgery, she embarrasses me with, "P*** off!" Now that's cringeworthy. Come back, Dad. All is forgiven.

She never swore when he was alive. If only my father hadn't got the dreaded 'Big C' before retiring, then I wouldn't be in this situation. Then, none of this was in my mum's plan, bless her. At nineteen, such attention-seeking behaviour isn't exactly my idea of fun.

"Wow, Mum, where did that come from?" I ask her when the dispenser enquires if she's been on medication before.

Mum nods. 'Oh, yeah! That Valium was good stuff, getting me through my bad patch."

She's winding me up. Then she makes an outrageous claim towards an innocent bystander, and I want to be swallowed up.

I splutter, "I'm so sorry. Mum doesn't really mean it," leaving our neighbour wounded. Meanwhile, her chaos counter rockets. My brother and I are still in our first year at Uni and Mum is supposed to be enjoying life.

Note to self: Marry early to avoid my kids going through this trouble.

Supermarket trips are swapped for home deliveries due to her outbursts. Even church friends are now making excuses. Apart from attending health appointments, she's limited to our home where I have temporarily moved back. Distance learning avoids her going naked in the street and more pearly bruises. I'm busy working on a junk mock-up recycled statue, towards my art studies that are light relief. Research is more difficult, especially when Mum is in full flow; a hand massage sometimes calms her down. At least I catch up on reading about art history while smelling of lavender oil.

So much for the precious year in digs – Leicester was wild during Freshers' week. Now a world away – a vast funfair and bar tours. Quickly picking up that the art scene was terrific, I hung around this fantastic art gallery until they gave me an installation to complete when sick of seeing me. But then, I stupidly offered to provide a sculpture to beckon visitors in. I must have been high.

That vibrant city excites me to think BIG. However, the prospect of the installation looming, with its cool launch, seems blood-curdling. Mum has to be a priority. The doctor mentioned her episodes are reoccurring bouts of depression. Having a turn, she grinds her teeth, chuckles, gets hungry, and sleeps. I try to feed her up. Initially, Prozac kept her decency editor on. She crushes my social life, though. Naively, I thought she'd improve. There's no way I'm letting Mum slip away as well. That would be unlucky.

Steve visits on Saturdays when I escape for my afternoon off. Having a licence, I go scuba-diving most weekends, to preserve sanity. On my brother's arrival, I pack up for a dive with my best mate, Rosie. He carefully pokes my stacked

The Real Me

cans asking, "What's this then, Sis? I see you've moved up from beach-combing," knowing it's my art project taking shape.

Becoming angry, I say, "I'm glad you're home to insult me."

"I doubt you'll brave this killer swell with today's high tide."

I ignore him. Diving is a no-brainer, though. Already the lunch table is laid with a fish pie bubbling. Mum's face beams.

"Thanks a million, Steve. Lunch will be ready soon. Can you make sure she eats something healthy? See you later, Mum." I give her a hug.

"She needs some meat pies, not this good-for-you stuff. Don't you, Mum? No wonder she's got sparrow legs." He turns back. "Make us a cuppa, will you?" Stalling mumwatch. She happily nibbles his chocolaty bribe while he shouts, "That sea's too rough!"

My twin forgets how well I know him. "No chance, Bro. It's your turn. I'm off." Still, he trails me, until I ask, "Guess what? Our mum was on antidepressants after we were born. I can't imagine why."

He shoves me saying, "Hurry back, Nicky."

"I hope yr ReD coz I nd 2 dive," I type to Rosie.

"BRT" is her reply.

When she is right there, I jump into the campervan singing, "Thank God for Saturdays!" I should get a spa treatment. Rosie wanted me to book that yesterday. As usual, I didn't listen; diving was the lifeline that avoided twenty-four/seven caring.

She drives down to Bay Scuba Club where diving empties my stress ashtray of all the rubbish stubbed out during the week. Nothing is going to spoil that. The crashing of the waves against the seawall gives me tummy flutters.

"Are you alright?" Rosie asks, checking my gear.

I nod, braindead, then take off despite my heavy tank. Limping into the water, the white wall of foam wafts a refreshing spray. We check out the surfers while pulling on our flippers, knee-deep in the froth. My heart leaps, revelling in sensory overload. The cold sends goosebumps to all those places outside my wetsuit when a rogue breaker causes brain-freeze.

Then, I bob back up hearing, "Arhh!" from amidst sandy swirls, fogging my mask. It exfoliates my face.

"I'm alive," Rosie shouts.

As her flipper clonks me, I'm swept back by the next white-wall eruption shouting, "Watch out!" We reach the small powerboat taking us to the buoyed dive spot. Tom's driving, and he warns about the conditions, but I insist. We plop off his boat with an agreed dive-time of an hour, sure of every inch of this coast where shale drops into a deep cavern. Adrenalin-charged kicks allow us to dive deeper to the calmer shelf where the wreck balances. The growling water clears of millions of bubbles as I descend, enjoying the super tingling; a natural mega-spa. My rusted vessel creaks reassuringly, her jangled greeting delivered via a planked backbone.

Appreciating her splendour, Rosie signals the 'OK' sign.

I give a thumbs-up, grabbing a timber, letting the old girl gently sway me while my buddy goes exploring. That's until I suck in and there's absolutely nothing there. Panicking, my chest hurts and throat burns... *Help!*

I'm saved by this spectacular mirage which begins with a clicking sound. My heart races as the swell of a huge, grey fish moves me. For a few seconds, I hold my breath, enjoying

The Real Me

the dolphin's hypnotic gaze. He notices my vulnerable state. During his ballet, this fantastic creature checks me out as sunlight bejewels his body. Playfully he turns, flicking his tail to help my stomach stop churning. Somehow, I gulp in breath again.

Rosie returns when her pressure gauge is low. She shakes me, seeing I have slid down the prop. My mate quickly swaps her secondary regulator for mine, and I splutter up salty water. Luckily, she's calm, indicating 'out of gas'. She holds me tightly, kicking on towards daylight to haul us up onto Tom's boat safely. Once reaching the sand, my buddy insists I rest. By this time paramedics approach the beach. Tom fixes that.

"The deal is that I'll go in the ambulance if you follow?" I negotiate. Rosie is ahead of me and out of her wetsuit, having grabbed my bag.

"Okay. And I'll let Steve know," she says.

"My bro will be pleased," I say sarcastically to Tom. "I owe you one." He blows me a kiss. He is adorable, but Rosie's welcome to him.

"TOUGH!" I hear her on the mobile. "Get real."

Sue, the paramedic, arrives to clip a monitor on my finger and ask awkward questions – like, "How long were you out of it for, Nicola?"

"No idea. It's Nicky," I add. "This is what happened. A dolphin knocked my trapped airline free with his nuzzle. He saved me!" Eyebrows raised, she checks my vital statistics, explaining the surreal does not impress her. Rubbing my forehead, she asks about headaches, to which I snap, "I'm prone to migraines, but then again I'm a full-time carer at the moment."

She holds her hands up. "I'm just attempting to rule out the possibility of a fit, presuming you wouldn't be diving with epilepsy. Right?" She gives me a minute, then, "Don't worry, we can do tests at the hospital," as the ambulance climbs the hill.

"That sounds fun," I say, "only, I've got to be back by five. My brother's looking after Mum, you see."

"I'm afraid that's unlikely. The doctors will want to keep you overnight for observation."

"You're joking?"

The driver called Jez wheels me into Minor Injuries. He's alright. I'm dumped into a cubicle to wait. Sue explains, "We'll stay until you're handed over." Although feeling sick, I don't tell.

"You know I'm fine now, really." I try to stand, but then feel giddy. Where am I going in that open-back gown? That's embarrassing.

"Not so soon, young lady." Jez lays me back. The doctor arrives and says he's running blood tests.

"We are monitoring your blood gasses," the nurse informs, racing around. "They're painkillers going through your drip." But by seven I'm in a ward for the night.

Rosie arrives. "Okay?"

I shake. Luckily, no one picks up on my fear. I'm scared that I inherited my mum's genes. Nodding off, Aunt Jane replaces Rosie who retreats for a shower. As it's dark outside, Jane pulls the floral curtain around my cubicle. A chicken sandwich and juice are delivered off the trolley. I'm quite thirsty, but give her the food. Then, feeling so heavy, I slip down under the sheet.

"I'll pop into your mum's on the way home to tell Steve. No problems. He will stay for a few days," she whispers. "There're things you ought to know about your mum. She hasn't always had it easy." And then she kisses my forehead, promising to be back in the morning with my washbag and a course book.

At the end of his shift, Jez drops by. He is cool. Lamely, I ramble on about my art background because he's easy to talk to. Of course, he isn't interested. It's probably his usual paramedic follow-up, so I enjoy him ticking his boxes.

Visiting hours comprise my Aunt chatting about the good old days. Going way back, a shocker comes: "This reminded me of years ago when your mum got muddled."

"Do you mean that she was crackers before?" Steve asks, continuing, "That must have been just after we were born," while passing a 'Get Well Soon' card.

"More like stressed out. You know that you two were premature. Well, that's just part of it. We didn't see your mum's anxiety coming. She only wanted things perfect."

I'm listening, I think.

"You know your parents needed the help of fertility treatment?" she continues.

Yeah! I heard that from Dad when I had sister envy.

"Dad told me that they couldn't face it again," Steve speaks for me.

"Well, there's more. The antenatal clinic worried that three babies would be too tiring, encouraging Mum's bedrest throughout." She hesitates. "Actually, one of their babies was given away not long after the births. It was supposed to be a temporary arrangement. There wasn't a network of support for young mothers with bad nerves then."

My mouth drops.

"It was all about coping. Later, your mum felt guilty for letting one of you go. Not an easy decision to make, but she took it hard. You had a sister, Nicky."

So, we were actually triplets? Making sure I got it. And, I have a sister.

"I hoped your parents would eventually explain," she confirms.

That's why Mum took Dad's death so badly; it unearthed more emotions. All this makes a monitor bleep.

Jane shrugs. "Steve heard this from your dad over a year ago, on his eighteenth birthday."

"What? I can't believe it." I shake my head.

Jane winks. "What's done is done!" As if everything is fine. The next few days are about more tests, and I'm allowed home, to take it easy. Follow-ups are inevitable, but I feel fine. Uni promotes recovery by granting extended assignment deadlines and supplying class notes.

However, my 'to do' list gets longer with finding my sister at the very top. Next, I reassure Steve, sitting with Mum at the Home, "My treatment is working."

He explains that to survive, he admitted Mum into the Sea View Nursing Home.

This weekend he made progress with, "I'm sorry!" The superb decking view out over the Bristol Channel is dreamy. Also, the staff have styled Mum's hair, and her nails are painted. Then he says, "Look how settled she is."

Giving her a kiss, I admit it would be useful if she could stay a while longer, prompting Steve to let out a gasp of relief. Again, he promises to be there but goes merrily back to his life. Meanwhile, I get a chance to take a peek into Mum's private paperwork. Jane pops in occasionally, and I'm tempted to sleep loads.

On Sunday, I manage to reach my mum. First, she calls my name on joining her in the conservatory. Steve isn't bothered about having another sister, but I am. So I ask,

"Can we do something?" Before the moment passes, she nods.

"Since I'm missing him, I want to ask God to look after our dad. If you don't mind, I want to pray that he's happily resting in heaven. And I'd like to pray that one day I'll meet my sister. Is that's okay with you, Mum?"

She looks up. There's a definite connection answering, "That would be nice, dear." Then, she shuts her eyes and relaxes. As I say a few quiet words she sighs, squeezing my hand. That's lovely; acknowledging the bigger picture gives me permission to keep digging.

Relaxing at home, we have a laugh. "Guess what? It seems Mum's care is down to me." Then Jane explains how my sister is back in Britain for University, after being brought up in Spain. Meanwhile, Steve remains clueless that I'm fixing our family.

Jane says, "You need to hold a family conference with your brother. I'll back you up."

"We'll see. Steve's got exams soon. I'll grab him afterwards." A break must come soon, but no diving is my dull prescription for the time being. Alcohol is off the menu, too. All that cabin fever equals a complete spoiler, giving coursework opportunities. Stuck in my sad existence, I need help when Mum returns home to convalesce. She can be quite sweet in between wandering.

Rosie came around that evening. "Do you know? My mum keeps knocking herself. I'm worried she's going to end up in A&E. They better not blame me."

"Nicky! You're getting your sense of humour back. I did miss you living in Leicester all last term, but you've changed."

"Yeah, student life's full-on. You'd love the Golden Mile shops; the Diwali lights are amazing. They stay up until after Christmas."

"I get that you're stressed." She knows. "I'll let you off if I'm still your best mate?"

"Stop it! You're my BFF." I give a high five. We laugh, pulling faces for a selfie.

"Love you, girlfriend." Rosie continues our teen reminiscence.

"I've missed you, but really, Rosie, I must return to Leicester before I get boring," I say, sounding serious.

She shrugs.

"This letter is my backup plan." I pass her an envelope marked Steffi. "Post it for me, will you?"

After I explain things she caves in. "Of course. If you're quite sure, that is?'"

I nod, excited to retreat to classes while Mum has got support. The new sophisticated me has a reputation, with Leicester ticking all the boxes. Being dynamic I fit into the arts scene by topping up on craft skills with short courses at the Art Centre. A Picasso dish on display inspires me to create in plaster. Still, I frown.

"What's up?" Rosie asks.

I laugh. "Nothing. Apart from my missing the amazing group of artists at the gallery, that's all. The exhibition is a collaboration of installations, including painting, print-making and sculpture."

"Oh, exciting! Is your mock-up finished yet?" She points to 'Recycled Rich' who brightens the kitchen with his foil quiff. "And...?"

"My study group reflected back on the photos I sent them. Creating a bust in plaster would be preferential. To

The Real Me

engage visitors, the sculpture needs to entice people into the exhibition. Well, that's for me to redesign..."

She looks worried, twiddling a lock of her hair around her forefinger – a trait that means she's tired. The soft strands matt like a rope. "Can I use your hand to design, please? Your finger needs to be pointing. Hold still." Before she does a runner, I whip out the roll of Modroc and cut it into small squares to go around her wrist, hand and a pointed finger. While the plaster sheets soak in warm water, I slap some Vaseline on her, which takes almost an hour to carefully cover.

While Rosie flips through my design book, I make tea for three. Taking Mum's tea as she snoozes, I rouse her whispering, "How do you fancy one of Rosie's farm's freshly laid eggs?" Watching her nod, my head spins, craving the old charismatic life. As Mum snorts, the contrast hits me of my study/home balancing act.

I creep out. Then, seeing my friend's puppy dog look, I cut Rosie's hand free from the cast. "That's great, thanks."

"All part of a best friend's service," she says, so I give her a hug. Trying to max out on my time, we play some music and eat sparkly cupcakes.

After, "It's just that in Leicester I'm somebody. You know?" I moan.

"Yeah, yeah. What's his name?"

"No, really. Actually, the staff at the Uni call me Nicola and they think I'm savvy. Can you believe it? Here, Mum ties me up watching too much daytime TV."

"And?"

"Okay, I found this cool guy called Finley because I'm using his six-pack for a mould of the sculpture's chest."

"Aha! So he and I will be close. Spill the beans about Fin."

"Well, he's interesting. It's not all about studying, you know. You have to be seen with the right people, in the right places." I blush.

"That's why you're playing it cool with Jez, I see." She elbows me.

"No, it's just I need to find my identity. There's more to me than meets the eye." She nodded. "Everyone knows Nicky's kind and Steve's clever. Lately, the tables are turning on the clever front..." Hoping that's true.

"Don't worry about it. You run back to your precious life. Just as long as I don't have to do your mum-watch."

"We're sorted, thanks. Jane has agreed to move in with Mum for the rest of term. I've got a plan now Uni is great with the extenuating circumstances. Actually, I'm heading back this weekend. Diving's off, so I may as well,' I regret saying.

She's gutted. "No probs. See ya later, then." Making excuses, she leaves, banging the back door and waking Mum. Who can blame her? I am a high-maintenance friend with dodgy genes.

Time-off finished, Mum is making the awful racket she does. Luckily the cooled cuppa is administered settling her. Soon I would make it up to Rosie with a proper invite to Leicester. The beginning of my win-win comes with the doctor declaring me fit. He agrees study is easier than mum-watch and arranges for some home-help. I don't bargain. Then, I gather my art stuff to limp back for culture. No more stifled creativity. Despite Recycled Rich being squeezed in the biggest wheelie suitcase onto the train, there was my new bust to finish sketching.

In charge, I bolt into the student life, making up for lost time. Discovering adoption papers in Mum's file back home has paid off. Getting in touch with the agency wasn't as

The Real Me

difficult either. They came back with excellent news. My sister is happy for us to make contact. My prayers are answered.

Meeting Steffi is amazing. I actually get to hug her, and we decide she even looks like me. Over hot chocolate in the student union, she reveals Mum's good friends first helped out, and then adopted her. We discuss the choices involved getting to know her birth family. One has moral dilemmas that Steffi should consider. Before she goes, she says, "Let me take a selfie," which feels fantastic.

I wait for her decision as energy levels drain during lecture-filled days while adding layers of plaster to the bust in the workshop during early evenings. Being on a runaway rollercoaster means doing research into a bronze statue called Flight. This is the steel one with curves that glisten outside the library. I love sculpting for hours deciding mine will be dark-skinned.

This fantastic showcase opportunity is proof of my competency. On the mobile, I say, "My new bust has been given the thumbs up. Please bring Jez with you!"

"You know I couldn't miss the unveiling of your Welcome monster. Who else is going?" Rosie encouraged.

"Oh! That's a surprise."

Planning the launch, Finley helps by making the slideshow of faces digitally taken from photos to project onto the bust. We add audio on repeat, "Your Gallery Needs You!" It had just been Armistice Day after all.

Finding time for Jez on the mobile, he nags about looking after me. "Failing isn't being second best, you know, Nicky." He ends the call with a test-results reminder.

Returning home Friday, for once there's no need to pop in on Mum. Jane supports the juggling of family commitments and keeps my sister secret. A red Micra screeches by

71

like Steve's, making me do a double-take, but the number plate reads "NAD".

Repeating, "N.A.D. If only." In medical terms, it stands for 'nothing abnormal detected'.

That must be a sign.

I look up. Thanks. Needing to trust things are right, I skip the doctors. Instead, I grab lunch with Jez to convince him that we are good. He's happy the gallery opening is approaching and lets me off.

When the launch date finally comes, Jez, Rosie and Tom all visit with Jane. I beam with delight when Steve and Steffi bring Mum in. It's great watching them enter the Centre and linger in the foyer to marvel at the familiar faces projected onto the bust. My Welcome installation is a success, complete with all my favourite people. The director is amazed, and I'm convinced my dad is smiling down, too.

Jez says, "I'm impressed you got everything done."

Making me laugh. Thank God for Steffi. Her help in covering the home front makes life manageable. "Bless you! You guys being here for me today is heaven sent."

Now, our future is sorted.[10]

---

[10] Published in *Klicbait Vol 2: Between this World & the Next;* edited by Alison Dunn, 2015 and read at the Writing for Liberty Conference at Lancaster University.

Love

IT MUST HAVE BEEN MY FAULT. THAT WAS MY first dreadful conclusion, on hearing the agonising news. Our family had been happy until this onset. Only, after those few foul words spewed out of a consultant's mouth, things changed forever. We were a young couple who thought we could have it all.

Why? Maybe it was the fault of the air pollution in ground-level ozone that I had recently found out about. We'd breezed into the Outpatients clinic but during the routine consultation my hubby went quiet. We just stared at each other in disbelief. Eventually, I fell into his arms. He gave me this hug then, "We'll be okay." Whilst holding back sobs, I leant on him. For Maggie, nestled between us, we simply had to cope.

On coming back into our cubicle, acknowledging Maggie the doc said, "Take a while to get over it, say six months and then try again. At least you know you can do it!" But then he labelled our poor, dead baby something horrible and booked me in to stop the night, to vacuum it away! Like, I was supposed to imagine nothing happened and be treated the same as mums who didn't want their babies! No wonder it did my head in. It was cruel being on the same ward with mums having abortions. They had a choice.

My dad came to my bedside to admit that it was sad. That something wrong had happened. Then, the surgeon discarded our unborn child and we were meant to walk away. Instead, we were shattered. Still, our toddler skipped happily unaware.

Back home, where previously I'd felt in control, that delusion disappeared. By forgetting our baby, we were expected to pull ourselves together!

The past weeks, a niggling meant Googling 'miscarriages' in spare moments. I hid this from Jack whilst battling to make sense of our loss. Seeking answers why our tiny baby had stopped growing, I resolved that there weren't any. Even after lots of tea and sympathy, "Accept and try not to blame anyone" went through my head. Unfortunately, at the same time, "Is it my fault or did God do this?" stabbed my heart. This argument was replayed at night. Meanwhile, life went on.

The baby clothes went away. More good 'out of sight, out of mind' stuff. An odd metallic taste in my mouth kept me from eating. Apart from the quick fix Galaxy bars that Jack treated me to. Mostly I stayed in. Doing a manic spring clean, despite everything. At the weekends Jack helped me with the big shop. He was hurting too. Long silences were every day, but Maggie distracted us. She was reason to carry on. The outside world was difficult asking, "How's the pregnancy going?" By us going across the road for tea, things blew up.

That's when I heard the dreadful, "Have you found that baby yet?" – a numbing question from our Rainbow friend.

Realising what her little treasure had said made neighbour Joanna crimson. "Sarah! What a silly question!" Her mother tried to smooth things over. Despite obvious cuteness, she'd relit the touchpaper, shooting jittery adrenalin around my bloodstream.

I interrupted, "No, that's okay!" Apart from pacing, then, "Honestly, you're alright, Sarah. I'm afraid my baby isn't actually coming back." More awful silence! Not their

Love

fault. Maggie was busy licking the icing off a bun. A quick getaway was my priority.

"These things happen all the time!" was Joanna's parting blow. By then I was having trouble. My heart was thumping.

When my sweetheart turned around to wipe hands, she giggled, "Maggie not a baby, me a big girl now!" Bless her! She assumed we meant her. I mumbled about bath night.

Rudely, we pulled on our coats with, "Come to us next time." Maggie rubbed her eyes; it was six o'clock before we collapsed through our door.

Jack was at the table enjoying five minutes reading the paper. My face said it all. He took Maggie off me asking, "Whatever's the matter?" Floods of tears fell, running upstairs. Plopping onto our bed, I muffled screams. Downstairs he sorted our daughter out.

When he came up, "It's not fair! What happens if I can't have any more?" I asked, like he knew.

"Stop it, will you?" He kissed saying, "We'll be okay." From my bedside table drawer, I pulled the only thing left of my lost baby. It was the ripped ultrasound picture I'd secretly peeked at each night. Amongst the swirls was this lovely outline of a head and a clear backbone.

I showed him. "Eight weeks scan. It was normal development, they said."

Jack's tear escaped. "You must stop torturing yourself, love. The doc says we'll be fine to try again soon."

"I know!"

"Well then."

Jack answered the phone. My sister, Elise, had arranged help. She'd booked a visit from our pastor, as we should have. Paul had done Maggie's baptism. Paul wasn't surprised. We listened whilst speaking sensitively about our loss and closure. He asked, "Why was there no funeral?" We shrugged shoulders.

Then Jack let it go. "You're having a laugh. We don't even know the sex of baby. We weren't told anything, in shock."

I shuddered, Jack continuing, "They said it was because the foetus was so small. Treating our baby as if he was a thing!" Paul patted his arm. I was relieved that he understood.

Paul suggested, "What might help would be letting go of false guilt." And, "You could try to forgive the doctors and God?" Seeing Jack's face flush, I nodded. Paul said it was no-one's fault. He read his bible. "Let's find the answers in here." We did, and it worked. We released dashed hopes by praying for reassurance that Baby was in a better place with an identity known to his maker. This made it doable. We would be blessed again. Reading, "You will have courage because you will have hope. You will take your time and rest in safety."

Jack said, "God knows what we've been through. He's seen his son die, too. What love!"[11]

---

[11] This won the 2010 Unique Writing Competition, and was read at the Lincoln Book Festival, 2011. Included in *Spiritual Awakenings* American anthology, edited by Sara Saint John, published by G.IS.G Heavenly Publishing, 2013.

Rosy

When we first moved into the old farmhouse
At the village edge, it had long since been falling down.
The buildings were picked over
    for anything remotely useful
But we got you and this beloved spot, out-of-town.

Under that dense canopy of your tangy pink blossom
We put up the decorated scout tent,
    to house a christening party.
New house new baby, or old house
    and me greedy with baby no. 3?
Either way Hannah came along to cheer us up, heartily.

So, hubby began the sure but steady job
    of home restoration
Whilst we enjoyed the fresh air, high ceilings
    and an open fire.
A set-aside garden patch boasted
    the old Reverend type apple
Onto whose strong, twisted bough
    he knotted a used lorry tyre.

Only just up the road from Newton's nature of gravitation
Where stands the famous flower of Kent eating variety.
I should have expected you, wise apple tree,
    to teach us much,
About valuing our long roots
    and the real importance of family.

So when the mobile veg man, Reg, said, "Cut it down,"

Count Our Blessings

Replanting we did but in an orchard much farther along.
Cos this aged tree held our kids in a swing for many years
Where we heard Han swish, as she rehearsed her song.

You reliably gave tasty fillings for our puddings
And I was grateful for your ever-honest stand.
You let her, along with her older siblings, safely climb
Against fatigue we will continue to have a battle, I find.

As you continue to share my changing burdens
I'm sure whilst our youngest leaves for University
By being the anchor for both laundry line and hammock
That time's just a number blowing over you and me.

So, if an apple a day does keep the doctor away,
We'll share the same spot, harmoniously.
Cos I'll not deny your chance to let your branches sway
Nor chop down or pull your roots,
    together we'll remain rosy.[12]

---

[12] This was included in a book of *Apple Day Poems,* produced by Sue Tapply, of the Handmaid Press, 2010

By the Grace of God Go Eye

I MUST ADMIT THAT BEFORE I KNEW HIM, I WAS A real worrier. My thinking was around being kind, but then I forgot to keep things in perspective. It was a pain. Luckily, Jesus wanted me to be more like Him. Change was good but took its time. I'm still a clay vessel in the potter's hands. He was very patient with me. Recognising His perfect timing meant that mine never could be... Lately, God has been testing my discernment. He began trusting me with secrets between Him and me, and several friends who requested *confidential* prayer. That was quite difficult – when sharing with others had previously been my default coping strategy. A problem shared was a problem solved, I used to say. Apparently, that did not count when the problem belonged to someone else, and then the only one I should share it with was Jesus. Then, I left the prayer request at his throne and stopped whittling. I needed to let God be God. I knew this.

At my daughter's summer wedding I read from Ecclesiastes 4:9-12. It said in those scriptures, "Two are better than one, because they have good return for their work: If one falls down, his friend can help him up. But pity the man who falls and has no one to help him up! Also, if two lie down together, they will keep warm. But how can one keep warm alone? Though one may be overpowered, two can defend themselves. A cord of three strands is not quickly broken." In front of a full church, it was time for me to stand by the words I endorsed. It was time to put my money where my mouth was.

So, my blessed life carried on. One of my favourite things is to wonder at the display of swans taking flight. A pair of such magnificent creatures regularly takes off on the canal nearby. Often the event could be heard before the aerobatic display of nature's miracle heavy-weight bird happened. The comical racket comes from violent flapping of wings and some hissing thrown in the mix. Usually, webbed feet slap with rhythm on the surface of their reed-filled runway as they accelerate maximising on cardio energy, to allow a steady uplift. Eventually, the commotion overhead is climaxed by a joyous blur of vast, white flapping wings. That is absolutely amazing, in my book!

Also, I find contentment in this gorgeous countryside around the Vale of Belvoir, where I enjoy a panorama of lush, swaying fields. There ladders of vibrant colour rose up after the storm. At first, emerging from the grey came reassuring blue sky; a promised ray of hope. This heavenly panorama extended in an arc of technicolour glory. I dared not blink for fear I would miss the watercolour progress. A bright yellow hue made me squint; I followed the colourwash sky unfurling across the fields. The palette of reds, oranges, greens and purples overlapped blues and yellows in meticulous order. Ever grateful for this boost of aerial vitamin C; promoting smiles that set me up for the sunshine ahead. However, above all, I cherished distinguishing the faces of family and friends. Whilst intimacy by touch was occasionally afforded to me, most cheered me with their smiles. These were precious gems twinkling throughout my day. They would lift my heart to giggle. So, that's why I was grateful for the gift of sight. Through recent tears in my left retina, though, those colours could have fallen away forever.

As a child, I was warned, "You'll get square eyes!" from sitting too near the TV or at the computer screen for hours. When the *disco* in my head began, I put it down to all of the above. Fair game, I had been charged and found guilty! Plus,

By the Grace of God Go Eye

I repeatedly inserted contact lenses in my eyes; another mythical no-no? I started the *blaming* thing. Even though, I was really trying to behave well. Whilst panicking, a headache with nausea crept in. An invading army of headlights marched across my vision, with hobnailed boots on. How to stop them? That was my pressing dilemma, after the initial sickening attack! Alarmingly, repeated high-visual performances scheduled themselves more regularly, albeit slightly lower key. Further stress-induced headaches were fought off by breathing through it. What followed was a run around the eye specialists, until the words "medical emergency" and "laser treatment" sank in. My future failed to avoid such certain eye-watering technology. Thankfully, there was help to stop the black curtain being drawn completely. My husband held my hand; he was praying. We trusted Proverbs 18:10, "The name of the Lord is a strong tower: the righteous run into to it and they are saved."

Listening to my body, which rebuked the first explanation of a sudden onset of migraine, I pushed towards a proper diagnosis. Rather than slate the initial medic's conclusion, I sought out a fresh Optician. His referral of my suspected eye anomaly certainly helped the process, from going on my instincts to the hospital consultation room. By God's perfect timing, I received specialist treatment to prevent the loss of my precious sight. The laser stuck my retina back in place, fortunately. Much respect went to Leicester General Infirmary's Ophthalmology Department and their gifted staff, plus Boots Opticians, Melton. Their intervention made a considerable difference to the appearance of my rainbow. I sent a 'thank you' letter to both of the consultants involved, Alex and Mish. Remaining positive was important.

It was not until the next time in church, when I sang 'The Holy and Anointed One', that His mercy hit me. It went like this, taken from Psalm 119:105:

> Your name is like honey on my lips
> Your Spirit like water to my soul
> Your word is a lamp unto my feet
> Jesus, I love You, I love You.

Then flowed tears of joy for answered prayer. Even when I couldn't deserve it, He went before me and provided. There followed confessions and further promises. A dear housegroup friend declared disappointment at being robbed of the opportunity to pray over my sight problem. When I'd been signed off from the hospital, I explained that I had such peace throughout that time of almost a year. It was only in giving thanks, that I was motivated to include the group. God had been there with me, throughout. It was not that I didn't need her prayers but that there were greater concerns to God, who already held me close.

Having faith meant leaving it at the throne of Jesus to sort out and not going ahead, blindly. I remained assured that He continued to be right there in my challenges, carrying me where necessary. Since then, she has shared a sensitive health situation requiring some more confidentiality, praise God! I was happy to shoulder that responsibility and offered it up in prayer, straight away. Only then, with wisdom from the word I took direction. Sometimes it meant being still and quiet. I've found the waiting an invaluable part of my journey and that God's answer was the best thing. I'm grateful that He provided all I needed, despite me being just me.[13]

---

[13] A thank-you note included online at the Voices Project, Christmas 2013

By the Grace of God Go Eye

"The pupil dilates in darkness and in the end finds light, just as the soul dilates in misfortune and in the end finds God."

Victor Hugo, Les Misérables

Our Picasso Dish

I saw an earthen vessel, just like me,
I saw juicy zest, leave a legacy,
I saw eagle-eyes, make wavy changes,
I saw currency, promise of wages,
I saw this artist, beckoning forward,
I saw progress come, in losing our guard,
I saw best practice, develop at last,
I saw experimental, improved craft,
I saw playful art, free-form *en vacances,*
I saw inspired work, tip the balance,
I saw refined art, despite any flaw,
I saw his gift, as symmetry for all.[14]

---

[14] This poetry was selected for *Welcome to Leicester, Poems about the City;* edited by Emma Lee & Ambrose Musiyiwa; Dahlia Publishing; 2016. Then a verse was included in Jo Fairfax's Nottingham Line of Light installation, 2017.

A Dot Deaf Legacy

SO FAR, SO GOOD! I PLACE A TICK NEXT TO MY daily devotional – "Be fruitful, multiply, and fill the earth and subdue it" – at the imminent blessing of becoming a grandma. Then I read, "God's command to subdue the earth and the animal life in it is a command to have mastery over all of it," which sets me thinking. As I can barely hold the excitement in, I ask my daughter to begin maternity leave with a day trip to a local arts centre.

She agrees, driving us to a local exhibition inspired by social and ecological issues. "The whole world is our responsibility," is my bumbling comment upon the artwork, as we wander through a gallery teeming with the best of British exhibits.

"Oh, Mum! But I'm at the stage of decorating a nursery. Please, give me a break." She finds a bench to rest while I investigate the magnificent animals until the performance starts.

Stroking her extended belly, I backtrack. "You know I'm here for you and bump, don't you?"

"Of course, I do. You're on babysitting duty when I return to work, and I'm counting on you!" Her baby brain focuses on the end game. She smiles as a cacophony of creature noises fill the gallery, exhibiting the 'Symphony for Absent Wildlife' installation.

"This is how Costa Rica sounded! It's eerie, isn't it?" I ask, as the diminishing sounds pause. It reminds me of last spring's rainforest trip when we travelled supersonically into fruitful forest linking our family's future. "You know... that's when Dad and I went on that kind of health safari. The whole area was full of these fabulous wild animals on steroids speeding around the canopy." Back to reality, we are drowned out by similar howls as the audio clip repeats.

She raises her eyebrows. "Oh. I just thought it was an exotic holiday on the beautiful Guanacaste coast."

"Admittedly, we stayed in a luxury hotel nestled beside protected rainforest running adjacent to the coral-filled Pacific." Warm memories come flooding back of clever, camouflaged insects we happily passed by, and vibrant neon birds we couldn't miss. "Your father got a brilliant snap of a couple of green and red toucans on the bumpy minibus journey up to the mountains." I clumsily flick through my phone photos but get sidetracked by some magnificent hummingbirds.

She recovers my attention asking, "Does it mean that the animal voices quieten the nearer they approach extinction?"

"I think so. And we need to protect the forests to avoid more species disappearing," I said, "but it's up to the individual to interpret."

She studies the space while I battle with the idea of my grandchild missing out on exotic creatures unless attitudes change. Noticing my frown, she talks of opening up vast swathes of wilderness to the curious traveller. I exhale the stress of worrying about issues beyond my brief. Relaxing by holding her hand sparks memories of medicines that oozed from abundant therapeutic fruits. Through the work of diligent researchers, I learnt it offered relief from Parkinson's symptoms. If the new compound could prevent my family from suffering, then I supported the development of this cure.

I remembered my husband's support: "To ease your symptoms, let's witness these magical seeds to celebrate God's remarkable provision." He enjoyed the Tamarindo Mountains where howler monkeys lived in their natural habitat. He loved the heat and wasn't disappointed with the variety of wildlife; only a short walk along the hotel's beach was a forested area full of white-faced monkeys and green iguana. Inland from that was prime ranching country with lean horses offering tourists rides along unspoilt trails. In this setting, it was easy to believe in miracles.

That's why we ventured up mountains by minibus, trekking up slippery steps in sweaty ponchos, only resting to admire exotic flora and fauna. Accompanied by zipwire-fuelled, adrenalin fanatic's screams, we pushed into the humid canopy, where our guide patiently showed us the source of the wonder drug. Remarkably, it hung from the rainforest canopy on rope-like vines. He pointed, saying, "Those life-giving pods are covered with whisker-like, stinging hairs. Beware!" My husband videoed my wobble on the steel bridge, nestled amongst treetops peppered with pods full of beneficial compounds.

Today, my hands still shake while searching for mobile proof. "What's excellent is that the legumes are nearly free from seed predators; the dense hairs discourage them." I convince our daughter, "So harvesting them for therapeutic properties won't upset the equilibrium!" I'm hopeful that the new drug will calm tremors.

She nods, explaining how state-of-the-art headsets are available to take us to threatened worlds by virtual reality to reduce our carbon footprint. To keep me positive, my eldest understands my desire to press for advances in Parkinson's treatments. Promotion of the drug advancement came from leaving a legacy in our will set up to extend medical research. Thus, life-saving compounds have the possibility of becoming a tablet. "We must respect the world's delicate ecosystems and maintain sustainability."

My daughter humours, "I suppose so. Let's splash out to celebrate at the café with tea and cake," avoiding any further conversation of family history.

My intention isn't to scare as we sip tea. "Did you enjoy it?"

"You mean the 'balance of animal life is tipped by man' theme? It's interesting."

"Yeah! It shows the vulnerability of those animals. Shockingly, tourists dug up orchids from the side of the rainforest road. Animal wellbeing depends on flora, agreed?" She nods, as I pray for a healthy baby.

"Don't panic, Mum! Somehow they'll preserve our planet for the next generation." My daughter carefully places a hand on her bump on top of mine, to allow me to feel her baby kick.

"There! I felt that one." A tear of relief flows.

"Life's not a rehearsal!" We hug.

Going home, I rub an achy neck after nodding off, until… "Wow, Mum! Isn't that rainbow amazing?"

Fabulous rays follow the rain to highlight heaven's promises.[15]

---

[15] Previously published in *Family Matters, an Anthology of New Writing;* Dahlia Publishing; 2019

Family Ties Go Beyond Token Gestures

A WINTER WEDDING IS ALWAYS FUN. FOR JESSICA and Luke, as teenage sweethearts, their first love tokens were friendship bracelets. Seven years later, a solitaire diamond engagement ring shows their relationship is serious. Soon, the sparkle from frosted holly berries promises to illuminate their fabulous occasion. Questions about getting to the church on a sledge are amusing at first. During their pre-wedding chat, when the vicar explains that the purpose of marriage is the covenant union of a man and a woman to commit to each other, Luke gets the jitters. Both are quiet on the drive home. The hall mirror reflects a pale complexion next to Luke's olive tones to remind Jessica to book hair highlights. When the groom produces the itinerary clarifying wedding plans, he liberally adds "weather permitting".

Despite earlier parental involvement, the bride worries her family are adding many of their own ideas. The couple must confirm arrangements with caterers, necessitating firm decisions. Once plans are agreed, her groom can tackle his family because being bombarded with questions from either side warrants a united front.

"Don't forget to mention we're serving a nip of sloe gin as an alternative to tea and coffee at the church," Luke says.

"Thanks! I'll leave that update to you."

"We can do this! After all, it's not quite the 'when Harry met Meghan' wedding."

Next day, after an early shift she broaches her parents showing them the top table plan. A high-pitched "Who's sitting there, exactly?" comes from Mum.

"Actually, it's a place for your granddad," the bride points towards Dad, who's called Henry. She winks at him. "At least, it's space for Great-granddad's notebook, so he's there in spirit." She recalls the quirky notebook contents.

"What a lovely sentiment – but you're joking?" Mum pushes her plate away to pace the kitchen. "You've instigated a memory seat when the wedding breakfast is already oversubscribed?"

Henry strolls back from the lounge where he retrieves his grandfather's nineteen-twenty notebook of tips for life, complete with business anecdotes. "Now let's not forget absent relatives, shall we?" He places the leatherbound book open on the kitchen table in front of him to read from "Tom". Dad reminisces using a posh voice, "'I have always made something, and there has been no greater joy or finer sport than being the creator of something… I hope this small treasure will help you.'" He looks up from concerns penned years ago for Henry's father, as a sick infant. This inherited advice can bless Jessica as she exchanges wedding bands.

"Don't be dramatic!" Mum switches off the radio carols.

Jessica longs for Dad to take her down the aisle in his new suit. This reassurance is welcome a month before she changes surname.

Dad indulges, "Listen, 'I hope you will have a wider outlook on life – get learning, get wisdom, culture.'"

"Tick, Jess already has them! Traditionally you toast absent friends in your speech, love. Let's avoid any controversy, Henry," Mum says.

"Hello! I like your style, Dad. Please, there's always time for going down memory lane."

Family Ties Go Beyond Token Gestures

Mum nods, encouragingly.

"The old soap factory was big business." Henry continues to read, "'Somehow, you find that life is a matter of cleanliness. You must do more than just wash. Your life must be clean as well, or your success will be limited to the time it takes to find you out. Do what is right.'"

"We're all good. I suppose he's saying cleanliness is next to godliness. Put that in your speech, if you like." Dad's eyes go watery. Jessica checks her watch. Meanwhile, Mum nips upstairs to ensure the roof light is shut from airing the gown hooked on its handle. Jessica hears the polythene cover protecting her lace dress rattling to scare off rogue moths.

Mum suggests, "Can I read from Ecclesiastes? That's with, 'A cord of three strands is not quickly broken.'"

Jessica smiles. "Lovely! I'll add those verses to the order of service."

"The notebook contents won't frighten Luke's family off?" Dad asks.

"Stop! We've nothing to hide." To delay a bridezilla flare-up, refusing to listen to whispers about the notebook's soap ingredients, Jessica leaves under an umbrella. Then, she drives to Luke's to give an update over a glass of wine.

Later, she produces fabric from a carrier bag. "What do you think about this fur for the bridesmaids' shrugs? I can easily run them up."

"Yes, they'll be ideal. Presuming it's faux fur?"

"Shut up! It's time for less meddling in *our* affairs."

Progress comes later that week when Luke meets his laid-back folks who suggest fish and chips and then ice-cream vans, to make arrangements simpler. They also spoil the groom by volunteering various last-minute wedding duties. He presumes Jessica is delighted with their proposals, so is in shock as she raises her eyebrows. He squeezes her hand. "If only I could read your mind, then I'd be more helpful."

She sings, "I'm getting married in the morning."

Relief comes when the wedding day surpasses all of their hopes and dreams. That afternoon the congregation happily buzzes with guests dancing until midnight to their favourite music from the wedding playlist. The couple congratulates one another on catering for everybody so well. Selfies show friends' cheesy grins, while the official photos capture the family celebration. Luckily, his brother takes a video for replay because the day flies by.

Afterwards, temperatures sizzle on their honeymoon to Elat where Red Sea dolphins choose to swim either side of the newlyweds. She interprets the mammal's attention as forgiveness of her ancestors. That's because years ago her family fished whales for blubber, to make soap. Jessica sighs, happily receiving the dolphin park escapees' karma. The couple kiss.

Once home, his mum texts asking whether they'd like to eat Christmas lunch at theirs. "However do we choose which parents to visit at Christmas?"

"We'll alternate!" Jessica declares.

"I suppose marriage works by putting each other first," says Luke.

Jessica has a lifetime to earn an eternity ring.[16]

---

[16] Previously published in *Family Matters, an Anthology of New Writing;* Dahlia Publishing; 2019.

A Delicately Laced Fingerprint

Indeed, it's right that
    I can't completely understand
what happened in the Lace Market
    from beginning to the end.
On a protected heritage journey planned,
    I made sense
from connecting with this
    famous industrial landscape,
to recount these interwoven
    'back in the day' memories.

Because today, in the footsteps
    of the great and the good,
following the Middle-Ages route
    taken from Nottingham Castle
by the legend of Robin Hood,
    I'm bound for St Mary's Church.
I'm in good company,
    standing on high ground near my birthplace,
Mary was rewarded for providing
    the firm foundation for all.

It's forty years since
    an old Stoney Street warehouse supplied
bleached cloth emblazoned with
    a classic five-leaf, floral motif.
There I completely identified
    with the Lace for Loveliness theme.
It was in the same week
    as Charles and Diana's marriage –

Count Our Blessings

that a stylish marriage gown,
    fit for a princess, was mine.

Then approaching sixty years,
    promoted to Mammar, I discover
many different contradictions highlight
    this ancient local history.
But I am just another,
    who stumbled across this High Pavement
to tread timeworn cobblestones
    around grand Victorian homes,
spied from twitched nets
    when madams wore scalloped collars.

Passing the sandstone caves,
    traditionally sheltering the hungry,
pulls at my heartstrings at those
    faded, noxious tannery efforts.
There lace turned from brown to white
    with dye, in basements.
Toil of that bustling trade was toxic
    for girls and children alike –
sweaty, back-breaking roles
    around hot, filthy lace machines.

When the original tram stopped
    for the Weekday Cross
at High Pavement,
    it was the preacher John Wesley who spoke
of the church as a boss;
    Hannah Guilford, a Sunday School teacher,
became Chairman of the Chapel Council,
    in 1904. Applying –

A Delicately Laced Fingerprint

"You are the body of Christ.
    Each one of you is a part of it."

Progressing from a British Empire's Hey-Day,
    market's stone lintels
told philanthropic tales above
    doorways to the lace storerooms.
That behind the Victorian mantles
    many had fine motor skills exploited.
Overlooked mothers who once powered
    a hosiery trade became
outworkers mending trimmings,
    as embroidered novelties declined.

Present-day stone gargoyles
    narrate battles over the use of remaining
warehouses swapped for shops,
    creative businesses and restaurants.
On the Walk, I'm wondering;
    Thomas Adam's schoolroom grew to a college.
Now, small stone flowers adorn offices
    to celebrate a conservation area.
Keeping faith was vital to cherry blossom
    our Contemporary paradise.[17]

---

[17] Found at the Nottingham Contemporary Museum, included in the 2019 Lace2Place immersive experience. Then, in the *Choice Gossip for Retail Later* booklet with Nottingham City Arts.

A Veteran Finds His Best Mate

WHILE ON ACTIVE DUTY, I GUESS THAT I GOT saved for a purpose. Back home, Faith was a regular giver who understood pain. She got me by noticing my signs of a recent return from conflict hell. Only, she was born with her limp. That could have been me overthinking things but as she treated me to 'meal deals', I needed her. Therefore, Faith was the angel who related to my everyday frustrations. My glass was half empty with shrapnel aggravating a crazed brain. At the same time, her glass was half full saying, "Thank God for my good leg!"

Many moons ago, desert sand clogged my weapon sufficiently to delay a final exit. Luckily, that military predicament was sorted by battlefield hero, Mike. He took a hit when my automatic jammed on tour in Iraq, adding to the guilt trip. By dodging collecting shrapnel for trophies, the rampant war remained in my headspace inducing rage. Today, the Old Dear's default mode was off track because as Nottingham's Council House clock struck two that made her late.

Recently, "Have a good day Bill," came after our agony aunt chat. Although Faith knew that my good day wasn't imminent, all empathy was welcome.

"Okay, cheers mate," I replied. She caved in at the pathetic stare of my scruffy greyhound, being a sucker for Midge. Then, she winced at my haunting flashback symptoms that resulted from cat naps. She agreed Mike deserved his medal, but my prize shouldn't be this miserable existence. I needed the works – Faith for luck, hope was gone then Mike got the glory. That was me summed up since the war. Peacetime remained a mystery.

A Veteran Finds His Best Mate

Only earning just over a pound on every copy of *The Big Issue* meant I tried being micro-entrepreneur. On that slow morning, blank faces ignored us with the first couple of quid spent on tobacco. A bitter night equalled stiffness. The lack of Faith appearing across the square indicated a broken schedule prompting debilitating spinal spasm. Few bought my magazine, even when I braved trams to wave it. "You've not bought a magazine from me, though!" I shouted at their glued wallets. Faith usually flitted from charity shop to my short-stay gaff in Market Square. The thought of losing another mate made me retch.

Faith was unlike the usual punters who judged ex-servicemen, though. During that particular week, after picking through sandwiches on their sell-by date at the minimarket, she warned, "Don't sell them on for drugs!" By handing over grub, she became the next assignment.

Hiding the crisps, Midge nuzzled, drooling. "Hold on, Midge!" We relied on her after binge-drinking weekends. I shouted abuse at the crowd; excessive pavement footfall prompted a turn towards the shop window to scoff. Faith was the diamond who wandered away avoiding confrontation realising my shakes were those of a soldier back from active duty. More protect and serve stuff – protecting her, serving me. I created a fresh home mission.

That fun afternoon, I lost it since her no-show. My hound had to pee, so I covered my sleeping bag with the cardboard groundsheet. Giving Steve the nod, I asked, "Watch my crib, will you?" Then, I shadowed Faith by tracing her usual route across the city. On overzealously trailing Faith up to the Castle gardens (Midge's favourite place to scrounge) during reconnaissance, I head-butted a rogue cherry tree branch causing intense aggro. Bent over, I snapped the branch to fling it. Pretending it hadn't hurt,

"Fetch Midge!" I blagged. Rubbing my head, I realised that an ancient battleground now had my blood added to the mix. That signal should have meant a stand-down, but military training overruled. Instead, pig-headed, I continued bothering the public.

Months later in court, they confirmed Faith's sainthood was the voluntary work of cleaning up the streets. She paid into society by befriending those no one else noticed. Because she couldn't make it to my hearing, I remembered Faith hobbling along across the busy Maid Marion Way, to share with Castle visitors about Nottingham's rich history. Lately, the castle had been closed for refurbishment. Bless her! In them wrapping up the castle walls to exclude visitors, she was redundant, too.

A song rattled my brain about being *"Beautiful"*, which had been inflicted on me by a squaddy in barracks. That bizarre, tuneful interruption made me check in with my solicitor from the British Legion. I had to know that lyrics hadn't escaped my mouth into the courtroom. Noticing my panic, the solicitor whispered, "All right?" On his thumbs-up, I relaxed. He'd persuaded me to wear medals, for sympathy. But this hearing wasn't going my way despite executing old soldier's mind games. Then he bragged to the court about my extensive peacekeeping service record. In response, Faith's barrister read her statement, how she was surprised at my out-of-character violent outburst. I squirmed, shamefully wanting to crack my skull on the wall and do them all a favour. Next up was the victim's solicitor who told the court how Steve was a regular Robin Hood.

I reddened in recalling. By trying a manoeuvre with dodgy radar from heightened senses, I attacked rather than appreciate Steve's non-violent manner. He only asked, "Can I give you a free haircut, mate?" But I took his generosity as sarcasm. Acknowledging my mistake, I felt sweat seep through my shirt to the suit jacket.

Stupidly, I remembered how I swore, shouting, "I'm fed up of hearing sh** about my dreadlocks. Back off!" Hearing the word "cut" alongside a flash of scissors prompted an automatic attack response. In the zone, I kicked off big time. As Midge barked my right fist tightened, and an adrenalin rush launched me forward to deck him. I roughed him up enough to leave him weeping, having removed his weapon. Content he was no threat, I happily jogged off to find the Old Dear safely sat on her orange wrap with her packed lunch. Midge sniffed her out. She went quite pale as I approached to tell of my dispute with the haircut clown. Probably, the bloodied scissors in my hand didn't help. Faith shook, packing up her stuff into her trolley when Midge accidentally knocked its contents over the grass. Then my soft dog ate her last sandwich. Due to this confusion, she said, "I'll pray for you. Now, I'm off to help the man you attacked."

"Stay away! He had scissors, for God's sake. You should take more care!" I misinterpreted.

Like a hero, Faith tried negotiating with a drunk who usually forgot the details of his exploits by the next morning. She chanted, "You know, I'm humbled that God allowed a thorn in my side." Was she talking about her walking problem or me? Unsure, I returned to the jabbering hairdresser. Feeling conflicted, I pinned him down before the local law came to peel me off. At the time, it felt right. Once more, my self-esteem plummeted on the home front. Not surprisingly, the police were cruel coming down roughly on me, despite surrendering the weapon. No one listened as they dragged me away, especially the barber. *Where has justice gone?* ran through my head as battle lines went blurry.

"Watch Midge for me, will you?" I shouted back to Faith. She nervously patted the dog, holding him back. The look of disappointment indicated that was a big ask then, thinking my people skills needed updating. So, I turned to the Constable. "I'm not fit to be around civvies anymore, am I?" What a relief it was to be locked up; the cells offered damage limitation. I was clueless of the trauma I was capable of inflicting going Maverick.

After a short detention at Her Majesty's Pleasure, and pleading with the judge, "I really regret my behaviour!" I explained, "I'm ashamed, and I apologise wholeheartedly for attacking barber Steve." As I scanned the room looking for that same guy, he returned a smile, weirdly. The judge nodded while looking at the charity worker's barrister, who explained from the victim's personal impact statement that his suffering was limited to temporary bruising. Generously, Steve didn't want to press charges. He got convinced I was in recovery from being under the care of the crisis team for those past weeks, on receiving a diagnosis of Post Traumatic Stress Disorder. His solicitor told us he'd been updated of this when the army doctor put the official blurb on the record. Like magic, the flagged medical information triggered essential support services doors to swing open wide.

Although having a label sucked, the persistent deregulation of body and brain chemistry kind of justified my outrageous behaviour. I winced at the accuracy of my present disorderly character. Also, Doctor said that healing was about rearranging my relationship to my physical and spiritual self. That was complicated. The referral to the Alcoholics Anonymous prompted another routine. Weaning

A Veteran Finds His Best Mate

me off sending angry texts to friends was healthier because they were vindictive. Expectedly, the AA experts prescribed exercise; like jogging to create endorphins along with some confidence training to help my communication skills.

"Thanks! I appreciate your leniency as I'm in a better place right now," I told the judge. "Don't worry. This veteran won't let you down. Faith wanted me to sort my life out, so I will. Also, you're giving me this break, and since being in proper digs, nothing but good things can happen. Really!"

Eventually, the judge turned. "Mr. William Machin, I don't want to see you in this courtroom again. Do you understand?" I nodded. He gave quite a speech about exemplary service that made me blush but finally handed out a non-custodial sentence and a curfew around Faith. A shaky hand was too slow to prevent the roar of laughter escape; my alter ego attempted more self-destruct, resulting from mixed emotions. He gave me a hard stare before the judge scratched his head and instructed me to write an official letter of apology to Faith. That reminder of the Old Dear's kindness prompted a guilty wave of nausea. It was all about her watching Midge. Hoping my hero was still active somewhere, even if I'd scared her off our patch.

Randomly, the judge warned Steve about appropriately approaching the homeless and suggested wearing an official lanyard to explain his charitable services in the future. Acting best mates wasn't a strategy he particularly recommended.

Finally, for my day in court the judge talked about the old enemy being a thing of the past. He made sure I felt discharged of prior official duties. The stressed-out muscles unknotted at the top of my neck at his refrain from locking me up. The winner was that war service eventually came in handy.

Although Faith wasn't in the room, she'd have been chuffed that I'd landed a temporary job in a charity shop. This win was the resulting no-brainer from having a proper fixed address. To prove that I'd changed, I wrote an apology note explaining how I tried to be more single-minded. She would know what I meant from our conversation on the street regarding the golden eagles on Mercian Regiment's infantry cap badge. Unfortunately, community service equalled the mind-numbing decorating of public buildings, for now. But an independent Castle tour went on my bucket list for essential social history lessons to resonate with my sad war episodes.

My future was brighter as the fight was over. Utter relief came when ordinary dreams gradually replaced those terrible nightmares. When I became fitter for decent company by unravelling the past, I shared, "War has no winners, you know!" Declaring this revelation at a meeting impressed the gals. The banging of this gong used to cause trouble with my army buddies, back in the day. These days, I handled conflict much better though. Peacekeeping was my present brief. By tiptoeing down a dozen steps, counselling helped to keep me sober. Sometimes I tripped up! Then, even in her absence, Faith's sound advice reassured. She must have left a guardian angel to watch over me to help uncoil the hyper vigilance; I went on a rewind. That was courtesy of a mega therapist encouraging me to relax then place bad memories to the back of my broken military brain.

Recovery was an absolute must to keep in the civilised society loop. To finally convince everyone that I was trustworthy, I must behave. I learned coping mechanisms that allowed me to function day to day. In realising that best mates quickly disappear, I hoped that Midge and Faith made a good team. It was up to me to build up a new team now. Faith showed how to give mates a break, and it was exciting to try doing the same.

By censoring me from sinking folk's company, true friends might understand. I had to find more courage to get out there amongst those who had got a grip on life. Their reality should rub off on me. This survival plan was ideal for the short term. More importantly, I had to learn to like myself again. That long-term goal was more difficult to execute, despite Faith's claim that Jesus loved me. Friends' compassion was the superglue.

Held up, I practised baby steps!

The Last Post – Turning Over a New Leaf

Taking my last walk in the country park
    just a few weeks ago,
before the gates were locked,
    I remained positive, even carefree.
If only I heard what the birds were manically
    chirping about then,
I may well have found myself doing
    the New Normal differently...

Instead our group of creative, middle-aged women
    – plus one gent! –
meandered, listening to wildlife
    and absorbing the wonder of nature.
As God's paintbrush swept a green palette
    to add browns, yellows,
then purple and orange hues
    graced a lawn of blessed crocuses.

Our intention – to observe the joys
    of Mother Nature on the hoof.
We bow below an arch
    taking time to hear the echoed swishing
of knitted, wiry willow branches
    thick with waxy, bursting buds.
To stroke a delicate sculpture
    as sparrows perch above, whittling.

I missed a blackbird squawk warnings

The Last Post – Turning Over a New Leaf

of a curved ball thrown
by an overseas wild species,
    including that variety of bat I find
had since infected us by sneezing out
    a cloud of the deadly virus.
We're hijacked by *no worries* fake news
    sent on the grapevine.

Absorbing germs, the treetop saxophone
    blew a loud melody
before the storm whipped up
    an apocalyptic, chorused gale.
In this vital outdoor space
    blessed by a cacophony of songbird,
little did I know, the denied right to roam
    prevented more trails.

To God, I'm thankful;
    He is the same today as was before,
and tomorrow the birds will sing along
    to their country dance.
Where you listen to sparrows merrily chortle
    from a sandpit,
the blackbirds shout a warning to stay away.
    No chance!

The branches knew about vital social distancing,
    even then
when humans were still sniffling
    the bitter pandemic scent.
Ash trees grew longer roots
    to help prevent their die back, so
we can learn from how

Count Our Blessings

    these wise, adapted fir trees bent.

Tomorrow, you'll touch and hug
    your family group and friends.
Please, gladly listen carefully to embrace
    everyone's perfect age.
Appreciate the birds' instinctive twitch
    to keep a safe distance.
Tomorrow is another day;
    try next *rebuilding your nests* stage.

Out of the mouths of those forgiven, wild species
    chicks live
so they fly in harmony with you
    together up to mature treetops.
Go raise awareness fairly,
    even on recycled handmade paper
until an unhealthy battle
    between creation and mankind stops.

Now, dig for victory
    while listening to climate change warnings
and I pray you live together
    to breath fresh air for another day.
This last post I leave you
    as a thought-provoking legacy because
my turning a new leaf prayer
    aims to sustain an extended stay.[18]

---

[18] This poetry went online at Edgehill University, in the Wow! Festival Lockdown, 2020. It is also in Leicestershire's Lockdown Digital Records and videoed for their record office time capsule.

Going Full Circle

As I navigate beyond middle age,
to anticipate celebrating the big sixty
I recognise life is not all about me
but more about me playing my part,
in an ever such more critical journey;
it's that of my precious family.

'Cos family is what glues us together
and family is what stands us apart.
To live faithfully to one another,
progresses us through our main events
and vitally, keeps us connected by
holding hands when we've sad hearts.

So, we love each other the same
as brothers and sisters from wide and far.
No longer does our past hold on to us
because we wear old chains no more.
Now, our future follows a true destiny
on which we can be entirely sure.

Believing God created us in His likeness,
then, old age is one of those privileges.
So thanks to grace, I'll pass on this love
as a gift of faith to the next generation.
Timely taking a turn to feel that I belong;
unconditionally, like throughout the ages.

And heaven is trusting in fantastic promises,
praying to complete the work for some time still.

Count Our Blessings

Therefore with patience, I continue to be
reassured of these amazing promises fulfilled.
Being assured of the dreams that match up to
the bigger picture; I'm a kind of natural.

Then, if eternity is a never-ending gift,
that lasts long after this fabulous life,
it's only made possible by a huge sacrificial fee.
Yes! The price has been paid on a cross for all
thanks to an unconditional love found there
that all equals a hopeful future, for this wife.

My 'New Normal' Schedule

SINCE THE UNFOLDING COVID-19 TRAGEDY AT-tempted to hijack my life, I counted my blessings. Recently, trying to listen to my inner voice blank out the bad news proved quite challenging. That was until I caught sight of a rainbow when, while helping me concoct a custard tart, our gorgeous grandchild asked, "Mammar, which came first, the chicken or the egg?"

My initial blurted response was inevitable: "He made both at the same time because God made everything!" That was before reaching for the Genesis stories from my bible. While remaining in hopeful mode from our cosy country kitchen-dinner, I considered the answer more carefully.

This was followed swiftly with the ever-present question, "Why?" It came from the nearly four-year-old. But I knew her parents would interrogate me further if I didn't explain thoroughly. So, I took my nurturing responsibilities in hand by sitting her on my knee and indulging in another cuddle. That was despite my hands balancing this toddler on a wobbly knee with her chubby hands covered in sticky flour. My gorgeous little Lily had dipped her entire outstretched arms deep into the large, ceramic mixing bowl to rub in the diced butter with her fingertips. That was until the pastry mixture resembled fine breadcrumbs without losing too much to the floor. Insisting she washed her hands once more while singing *Happy Birthday* had interrupted her interest in the bake. Recent emergency habits remained. That's when my mind fluttered away to the times my children used to help me bake on the Aga, back in the old farmhouse kitchen.

As I glanced out of the window over the garden to the neighbour's farmhouse, I reminisced of being a parent back in the nineties. That's when I had five hungry mouths to feed on a smallholding. I told Lily about how we kept a chicken coup of our own for many years, while living next door. She looked confused, having seen the mantelpiece photos of her mum and dad standing outside the old farmhouse before; we stared out. Going back, I explained the delight of her mum and siblings in feeding the hens grain and in particular, collecting the eggs. Then, I remembered their excited squeals of, "This egg is huge! I'm having this one for my tea 'cos it's definitely a double-yoker!" I laughed, recalling our family history of how her uncle was chased by a cocky cockerel, which had to be banished out the village when it got aggressive.

Thus, I pointed over to our greenhouse to say, "That's where the coup used to be."

The tiny chef made comforting 'Oh, I see!' sounds in response to our family history. She slipped away munching on a chocolate biscuit. Reflecting how hard it was to work the land, I craved my grandchild's boundless energy. From spotting the cat on our lawn through the back door glass, she ran into the garden to travel up and down the slide numerous times. Out there in the open air she was free. As I waited for the pricked pastry that I'd just lined in a tart tin and placed in the oven to bake blind, watching her from the kitchen window, my mind locked onto when the kids all left for University. This was around 2010. Triumphantly, I congratulated myself, nodding that we downsized for a good reason; once we realised the children were not returning home. Then, Dad and I had reflected that periods in life happened for a season, so we embraced our empty nest stage. Call our season of change a lightbulb moment. To tell the truth, after more than twenty years of stability, neighbours feared my builder husband and I had completely

My 'New Normal' Schedule

lost the plot. As if we were in full flow mid-life crisis, they backed off while we adapted to preparing smaller feasts from an adequate plot. However, during the decluttering of old pots and pans, my godmother muse flew in. By 2014, kinder locals would call me quirky. My imagination sought joy over the muddle, that's all.

Meanwhile, that baking day, Lily burst back into the kitchen smelling the pie case from outside. Her nose sniffed enthusiastically asking, "Can I eat some yet?" I shook my head when my thoughts wafted back in the room on a blast of fresh air. As I wiped surfaces and used the mixer, she covered her ears at the noisy blending of the eggy filling. She had just triumphantly cracked open and stirred several free range eggs into the mixing bowl. When I heated the milk, vanilla essence and sugar in a small pan until nearly boiling, she chatted along to her doll. Lily then watched me pour the mixture over the beaten egg, stirring continuously. She loved sprinkling over a little nutmeg. There was spare pastry so we crisscrossed the top of a small strawberry jam tart with thin, cinnamon-covered pastry strips for a treat. Finally, back to the oven, we left the custard tart to bake for an hour at a cooler temperature, until set. Those comforting wafts of pie smells prompted more of those valuable daydreams.

As our grandchild explored the sandpit on the patio, I sat near the open door listening to her chat along to her doll. I managed to get my breath back by cherishing homely memories of just a few years earlier. That was when I wrote a note to self in a diary: "Listen to your heart for guidance." My meaning was, it was my time to shine by expanding horizons. And through maintaining flexibility on approaching the age of sixty, I created my real-life adventure story. For years, as a couple, we were too busy to think about life choices. We simply had to get on with the day-to-day chores presented in that turbulent rural setting. Admittedly, I enjoyed peddling the worthwhile treadmill of providing for a family. This essential time was exhausting with three lively children making colourful jottings, yet I would not have had it any other way. Then, it got scary because too many options threatened to blur my security lines. Time on my hands proved scary back in the day, similar to how it was on lockdown.

Then having survived the indignity of angry teenagers, I celebrated two daughters working within the National Health Service, and an engineer for a son. So, over the last decades, my husband and I achieved relevant hard copy through them. My possibilities were enlarged by tweaking how precious moments were spent, rather than becoming a slave to routine, including tending the garden. I had a whole world of flora in which to flourish. Promised a banquet of housewarming barbeques, Dad concentrated on converting our new home to a small palace while slowing down his work pace. We listened for pointers leading in the right direction, shying away from old habits. We attempted to model a rewarding lifestyle less dependent upon money and more self-sufficient. We desired to be helpful using our work experience from our converted garage at the bottom of the garden. It was all very cosy.

At that same time, my butterfly brain realised, since making a diversion to a more relaxed schedule, we adopted the premise of *anything is possible* to steer new chapters, along exciting paths. Our late availability offered the potential for enormous excitement and some trepidation. Once, I sought guidance from our adult children about this over Sunday lunch. I remembered their procrastination: "You know if I were a cheese I'd be the local full-bodied, creamy Stilton."

My 'New Normal' Schedule

"Do you mean ripe?" my son joked.

"Not quite that, you cheeky thing! I mean more like the local, blue-veined mature variety that is complimented by a glass of red wine. Haha!"

"Oh, Mum! That's too deep," my daughter accused me, as ever the sceptic.

"But while in specific settings I'm still palatable, I'm fast approaching a 'best before' date! My clock is definitely ticking..."

"Listen to your mum's ideas, will you?" my hubby interrupted.

"To be fair, preserving vintage flavour requires the addition of a distinctive kick." A younger muse was seeking its stage.

"What are you up to exactly, Shirley Valentine?" was our daughter's question.

Then I replied, "Our future is not up for debate. It's just that for the first time in years, I'm no longer just someone's mum or teacher. I'm thinking about the best outcome despite certain health restrictions your dad and I face. We need more hammock time."

Dad agreed. "This time before grandchildren come along, could be an amazing chance for both your mum and me. Don't you see?" They responded with raised eyebrows, then shaking their heads before dispersing home.

When letting go of many former, vital clunky bits of trivia besides our family home, I returned to tend the people that came on loan. That paring back experience was liberating but not altogether popular!

During that decade of re-evaluated years, my daily word count was on track. Although still a wife and homemaker, lame excuses for remaining tied to the kitchen held no weight. Extending my reach to beyond our patch was a goal.

113

Empty nest success was about me being the scribe rather than our circumstances doing that for me. Dad got his time to shine cooking tasty Sunday dinners and took up more outside hobbies. His allotment grew to feed some of our extended family. Also, despite independence from offspring, I decided that if I did not make my schedule, then parents and siblings would happily fill my days with odd culinary jobs. Our good news was not achievable until some exciting travelling and exploration had happened. A few long faraway shore holidays opened our eyes to the bigger picture about the environment. Fresh aspiration teased me forward for boldness in action to spearhead fulfilment.

So, I reflected that my independence blossomed. In stepping away from a humdrum routine, in an attempt to revamp me, carefully considering my timetable was well worth contemplating. The slow cooker was dusted off, and I bought free-range eggs locally. We generally smelt the roses by swimming and doing charity work. Since I had metamorphosed into this laid-back woman of leisure, along popped out a grandchild to bring some of the old me back and increase the pace somewhat. There reality kicked back in! My muse happily skipped into picture book colours when tiny feet pattered by a couple of years ago. New activity was varied, including the physically demanding swing push. My subconscious had time to rid itself of useless blurb to concentrate on the shared practical business of rearing another generation.

Moving on in my attempt to bake a decent egg custard, toddler Lily was wiggling, indicating that she urgently needed the loo before we removed the tart from the oven. Waiting to wipe, I thought that along the way, familiar pastimes were swallowed up but that over all we had made the most of time. When I shared about resting upon, "I walk

My 'New Normal' Schedule

by faith and not by sight," life got more comfortable. Fuller lifestyle was still about making sacrifices, but the win was increased availability that led nicely to unveil an energising family drama. So, moving to the bottom of the garden was reflective of a semi-retirement restructuring plan that worked for us. Our youngest daughter even accused us of becoming *Poddington Peas,* by living at the bottom of the garden, after some cartoon characters. I read Lily the picture book to explain the concept of therapeutic downsizing to sever our reliance on former irrelevant pressures, in a fun way. All we did was to hop off our hamster wheel for survival. To friends asking us over for lunch we often said, "We've never been busier now the sunny days are upon us. However did we manage to work full-time?" Rescheduling offered huge health rewards; its official that grandchildren kept us fit by buggy-pushing. With tending a fruit and vegetable patch we slept soundly.

That day not so long ago, Lily kept me grounded admiring her bake asking, "Mammar, why is the jam in pie-prison?" Referring to the latticed pastry on top of the jam tart, I mentioned the necessity for chickens to be kept behind wire, for their safety. Noticing her frown, I skipped the harrowing but real 'fox culling chickens' episode. Maybe when she was older, I would share that one. We had been through enough recent traumas with the virus. Now, life was all about joy.

Instead, I asked her, "Which one do you think came first, the chicken or the egg?" Then, together we Googled it. We giggled tasting our delicious eggy pudding. When her mum picked her up, Lily told her about chickens being the winners in the race.

My daughter asked, "Have you been filling Lily's head with stories again?"

A recent unlocking of chains helped me be okay with that accusation. "Yes! I absolutely have! Chameleon-like, I learned to merge the best of the old life stories with the new to discover equilibrium. One day, you might try it?"

Nowadays, I worry less about borrowed time. As our past and present stories merge, each day of sunshine is a real bonus in this new normal.

Surviving Groundhog Day with the Cross

Since the heroic, frontline example is finely drawn,
I try to emulate the NHS's diligent responsibility.
And during these essential lockdown days of ours
I record a chronological time, alongside frivolity.

Each morning, I wake to an enthusiastic promise
from hopeful tracks, urging me to walk in test stages.
As motivation to lift my eyes and keep on going
with a God who supplies hope, through all ages.

From day one, our activity adheres to a routine;
even as the cord is cut, we are told to toe the line.
Feed time, nap time, from play zones to learning
until, at school an entry assessment is the baseline.

Older folk rely on less steady, addictive props –
of confusing lines we are warned to avoid crossing.
Still, when anxiety grips, instead of manning-up
we often try blurring the fearfully disappointing.

So, I'm thankful to those lifelines that keep us safe.
Since the Covid zigzag hijacked normal activities
we wash our hands and practise socially distancing.
Yearning for a promised return of gathering pleasantries.

Earnestly I seek in prayer the punchline for 2020.
Moving on from the trauma of this pandemic bug
before final moments come for my beloved, I go

beyond fingers crossed, to Him, for granting hugs.

As new normal is threatened by old distractions,
"Spare me and mine as well as your saints," I plead
to a merciful Father, who weighs my needs fairly.
Thus, I stay vigilant to cross over on my knees.[19]

---

[19] In Leicester's Museum and Art Gallery's 'Inspired in Lockdown' exhibition, September 2020 - present day.

Horses for Courses – A Letter to my Younger Self

FORGIVE ME FOR NOT WRITING EARLIER ON THIS taboo subject of hormones. They are to be respected, believe me.

I remember the time you started a journey into wild womanhood, thanks to those dreaded chemicals stimulating fiery reactions throughout your veins. We say horses for courses, don't we? At home, hooves were firmly planted in grassroots – they led you out of the stable on a short rein. When you escaped, you protested with loud snorts and many a whinny. But bets were off as you cantered towards maturity. It was as if puberty were to be jumped over, at all costs.

As a filly bolting out of the starting gate, you were raring to go. You watched the stallions pass you by until successful introductions came from the careful steering towards a more mature breeding stable. As a mare, you sweated excitedly towards the finish line of a thoroughbred breeding course, gaining steady experience with a sure winner at 3 to 1. He was your Mr. Right.

On your mark, you married and triumphantly waited for the rosettes to be pinned to your scoreboard. In your heyday, you were blessed with strapping offspring to successfully compete with. Your first rosette, red, came with the birth of your first child. That initial race was won with ease. Sadly, in the next race, you fell at the first hurdle and had a blue time with a non-starter. A yellow rosette came swiftly after, followed by a green, and your stable of three beautiful children was complete thanks to those pesky hormones. I'm delighted to say, long after the shot reverberated around the track, you kept running. Three grandkids have subsequently joined the fold, your happy family the best trophy of all.

Since menopause, hormones still bamboozle your mind. You're quirky, but that's no wonder, what with lowered levels of oestrogen and testosterone acting as secret double agents. These pit ponies were never sure bets. Even now, they regularly send security messages to your trembling body to comfort eat. Watch out for lameness because you no longer need that same old rush to get a buzz.

Despite these up-and-down covert pulses, hormones sustain, strengthen, maintain and even repair. They were a pain for many years, adding unwanted whiskers and dreadful bone aches, but more recently they're on your side.

It's no surprise that you are perplexed contemplating the hormonal love/hate relationship. But as you steadily pick up on life's hazards and hurdles, adjusting to the pandemic lockdown crazy should be doable. After trotting in a metamorphic state to beat this national insecurity of high-risk poison, managing hormones is okay. There will be no break in the races today.

Finally, as you approach the finish line and before you are put out to graze, stay in service of a creator God. Remember, it was He who graced you with that renewal kick.[20]

---

[20] This was written for a 2021 anthology at Writing East Midlands, after 'The Silent Archive: Let's Write about Menopause' workshops.

Also by Fiona Linday

Get Over It
Published by Onwards and Upwards
ISBN: 978-0-9561037-7-2

"Earlier that month, back home, I wasn't completely fazed when it dawned on me Mum couldn't make it. I should have known. Anyway, since then I agreed to come along to help my dad out. But I didn't want to come. I was doing him a favour, although why I should, I really don't know. After all he's never done anything for me."

Get over it? How could I? The main person in my life was gone… forever.

Available from all good Christian bookshops
and from the publisher:
www.onwardsandupwards.org/**get-over-it**

About the Author

Fiona is treasurer of Scriptorium, an Association of Christian Writers Nottinghamshire affiliated group and also a member of the Society of Authors and the National Association of Writers in Education. She first wrote the young adult novel *Get Over It*, published by Onwards and Upwards, in 2009. That was read at the Nottingham Arts for Change with Renaissance One. Shortly before came her prize-winning short story, *Off the Beaten Track*. Then, she won the Unique Writing Publications Short Story Award with some prose non-fiction entitled *Love* in *Spiritual Awakenings, Stories of Praise & Redemption*. Afterwards, she published an eBook anthology called *The Heavenly Road Trip*. Included in the *Welcome to Leicester* poetry collection with 'Our Picasso Dish', she also edited *Family Matters, an Anthology of new writing* at Dahlia Publishing. In that 2018/19 Arts Council England supported anthology writing project she collaborated with learners from Attenborough Arts Centre, Leicester University.

Several of her stories and poems are included in anthologies. See www.fionalinday.co.uk.

To contact the author, please write to:

Fiona Linday
c/o Onwards and Upwards Publishers
4 The Old Smithy, London Road,
Rockbeare, EX5 2EA